HEBREWS

DISCOVER TOGETHER BIBLE STUDY SERIES

Leader's guides are available at www.discovertogetherseries.com.

DISCOVER TOGETHER

BIBLE STUDY

HEBREWS

*Discovering a Better
Fulfillment in Jesus*

*Sue Edwards
Rebecca Carrell*

KREGEL
PUBLICATIONS

Hebrews: Discovering a Better Fulfillment in Jesus
© 2025 by Sue Edwards and Rebecca Carrell

Published by Kregel Publications, a division of Kregel Inc., 2450 Oak Industrial Dr. NE, Grand Rapids, MI 49505. www.kregel.com.

Library of Congress Cataloging-in-Publication Data
Names: Edwards, Sue, 1947– author. | Carrell, Rebecca, 1974– author.
Title: Hebrews : discovering a better fulfillment in Jesus / Sue Edwards, Rebecca Carrell.
Description: First edition. | Grand Rapids, MI : Kregel Publications, [2025] | Series: Discover together Bible study series | Includes bibliographical references.
Identifiers: LCCN 2024037200
Subjects: LCSH: Bible. Hebrews—Textbooks. | Bible. Hebrews—Study and teaching. | Christian women—Religious life—Biblical teaching.
Classification: LCC BS2775.55 .E39 2025 | DDC 227/.870071—dc23/eng/20240930
LC record available at https://lccn.loc.gov/2024037200

ISBN 978-0-8254-4898-0

Printed in the United States of America
25 26 27 28 29 30 31 32 33 34 / 5 4 3 2 1

Contents

Why and How to Study the Bible

Varied voices perpetually shout for our attention. Whose voice deserves our trust? The politician or evangelist on television? The Wall Street CEO? The Uber driver we've never met but count on to take us home? The man hawking cell phones behind the counter? The woman on the treadmill beside us? Maybe we can trust them; maybe we can't. Over time we can discern whether or not we're comfortable inviting them into our personal space or giving weight to their opinions. But reality reveals that in time, everyone will disappoint us, and we will disappoint them.

Only God is perfectly trustworthy. Only God offers authentic hope. "Therefore, with minds that are alert and fully sober, set your hope on the grace to be brought to you when Jesus Christ is revealed at his coming" (1 Peter 1:13).

Years ago a wise woman, who secretly paid for my (Sue's) daughters to attend a Christian school we couldn't afford, planted that truth in my mind and heart. This concept blossomed into realistic expectations for life and a hearty hunger for a relationship with that perfectly trustworthy one. That hunger led to a lifetime of savoring God's Love Letter, the Scriptures, and that relationship and practice upended everything. Wherever you are in your journey, Jesus invites you to experience abundant life with him. How?

Together let's discover what the New Testament book of Hebrews reveals about why, above everything and everyone else, Jesus is better.

How to Get the Most out of a Discover Together Bible Study

We're all at different junctures on our spiritual journeys, but God's Word doesn't separate us according to superficial differences. We all want to know God intimately and flourish, and we can all learn from one another. "As iron sharpens iron, so one person sharpens another" (Proverbs 27:17).

Discover Together Bible studies are designed to promote unity, for all women to learn from and enjoy one another regardless of age, stage, race, nationality, spiritual maturity, or economic or educational status. God proclaims we are all sisters in his forever family, preparing to spend eternity together (Matthew 12:46–50).

However, our schedules vary week to week depending on the needs of loved ones, travel responsibilities, and work demands. To honor these differences, this study provides two choices:

1. Basic questions that require about one and a half hours of prep a week, offering in-depth Bible study with a minimum time commitment.

2. "Digging Deeper" questions for women who want to probe the text more deeply.

Women wanting to tackle the "Digging Deeper" questions may

- need resources such as an atlas, Bible dictionary, or concordance;

- check online resources and compare parallel passages for additional insight;

- use an interlinear Greek-English text or *Vine's Expository Dictionary* to do word studies;

- grapple with complex theological issues and differing views; and

- create outlines and charts and write essays worthy of seminarians.

In addition to God's Love Letter, we also need authentic community and a place to be ourselves, where we are challenged to grow and loved unconditionally despite our differences.

This Bible study is designed for both individual and group discovery, but you will benefit most if you complete each week's lesson on your own and then meet with other women to share insights, struggles, and aha moments.

If you choose to meet together, someone needs to lead the group. You can find a free downloadable leader's guide for each study, along with tips for facilitating small groups with excellence, at www.discovertogether series.com.

Choose a realistic level of Bible study that fits your schedule. You may want to finish the basic questions first and then dig deeper as time permits. Take time to savor the questions, and don't rush through the application.

Read the sidebars for additional insight to enrich the experience. Note the optional passages to memorize, and determine if this discipline would be helpful for you.

Do not be intimidated by women who have walked with the Lord longer, who have more time, or who are gifted differently. You bring something to the table no one else can contribute.

Make your study a top priority. Consider spacing your study throughout the week to allow time to ponder and meditate on what the Holy Spirit is teaching you. Do not make other appointments during the group Bible study. Prioritizing time with Jesus exhibits that he is truly your first love (Revelation 2:4). Ask God to enable you to attend faithfully.

Come with an excitement to learn from others and a desire to share yourself and your journey. Give it your best, and you'll find the only one who will never ultimately let you down or leave you.

WHAT IS AN INDUCTIVE STUDY AND WHY IS IT SO POWERFUL?

The Discover Together series uses inductive Bible study as a structure to dig into the Bible. *Inductive* means using specific observations to determine general principles. Inductive study is the practice of investigating or interviewing a Bible passage to determine its true meaning, attempting to leave behind any presuppositions or personal agendas.

First, we seek to learn what the original author meant when writing to the original audience. We carefully examine the words and ideas. We ask questions like, What is happening? Who is it happening to? And where is it happening? Only after we answer those questions are we ready to discern what we think God meant.

Once we are clear about what God meant, then we are ready to apply these truths to our present circumstances, trusting that a steady diet of truth will result in an enriched relationship with almighty God and beneficial changes in our character, actions, and attitudes.

Inductive study is powerful because discerning biblical truth is the best way we grow in faith, thrive in our lives, and deepen our relationship with the God who created us.

To experience this powerful process, we must immerse ourselves in the practice of study as a lifestyle—and not just focus on a verse here and there. Our life goal must be to digest the Bible, whole book by whole book, as life-giving nourishment that cannot be attained any other way.

Over a span of sixteen hundred years, God orchestrated the creation of sixty-six biblical documents written by the Holy Spirit through more than forty human authors who came from different backgrounds. Together they produced a unified Love Letter that communicates without error God's affection, grace, direction, truth, and wisdom. He did this so that we would not be left without access to his mind and heart.[1]

THE INCREDIBLE BENEFITS OF BIBLICAL LITERACY

Earning a quality education changes us. It makes us literate and alters our future. Many of us sacrifice years, money, and energy to educate ourselves because we understand education's benefits and rewards.

Biblical literacy is even more valuable than secular education! But just like with secular learning, becoming biblically literate requires serious investment. However, the life-changing rewards and benefits far outweigh a diploma and increased lifetime earnings from the most prestigious Ivy League university.

A few benefits to Bible study include

- a more intimate relationship with almighty God;
- an understanding of the way the world works and how to live well in it;
- a supernatural ability to love ourselves and others;
- insight into our own sin nature along with a path to overcome it, and when we fail, a way to wipe the shame slate clean, pick ourselves up forgiven, and move on with renewed hope;
- meaning and purpose;
- relational health experienced in community;
- support through struggles;
- continued growth in becoming a person who exhibits the fruit of the Spirit: love, joy, peace, forbearance, kindness, goodness, faithfulness, gentleness, and self-control (Galatians 5:22–23); and
- contentment as we learn to trust in God's providential care.

Every book of the Bible provides another layer in the scaffolding of truth that transforms our minds, hearts, attitudes, and actions. What truths wait to be unearthed in the depths of the book of Hebrews, and how will they change us?

Why Study Hebrews?

TO KEEP US FROM SETTLING FOR SECOND BEST

Do you ever look back over your life and wonder if you are settling for second best?

You meant to remain committed to the Bible study, but your friend suggested you attend a yoga class together. It met at the same time, and you couldn't resist the dual temptation of catching up with her and toning up those bulges.

You had every intention of finishing your Bible lesson, but a text popped up reminding you that those shoes you love are finally on sale. Better get there before your size sells out. Now it's too late, and what would others think if you attended without adequate preparation?

You finally signed up for that church class about understanding the Bible, but your unbelieving neighbor knocked on the door just as you were about to leave, needing your help with a project. You'd feel guilty not helping her, even though you're clueless about directing the conversation toward spiritual topics.

Friendship, exercise, frugal stewardship, loving and witnessing to our neighbors—all are good ways to live out our faith, but can they woo us away from the "best"? It's the "best" that ultimately enables us to interact wisely with friends and nonbelievers, develop self-control that leads to good health habits, and learn principles of good stewardship that enable us to use our resources well for a lifetime. The best informs the good, resulting in joyful maturity and skill in living.

Jesus's interaction with Mary and Martha illustrates that the temptation to settle for second best isn't new. When they opened their home to Jesus, Martha busied herself with all the necessary preparations, while Mary sat at Jesus's feet, in the posture of a disciple. She knew not to allow the good to crowd out the best. And Jesus affirmed her decision as he gently chided her sister, "Martha, Martha . . . you are worried and upset about many things, but few things are needed—or indeed only one. Mary has chosen what is better, and it will not be taken from her" (Luke 10:41–42).

It's not easy to navigate the Christian life wisely, discerning between the good and the best, especially when God's Word instructs us to love him with our minds, hearts, and hands. But God didn't leave us helpless as we attempt to make the best choices in life. That's one of the reasons the Holy Spirit included the book of Hebrews in our Bible. It's designed to guide us so that we never look back and wonder if we've settled for second best.

TO INFUSE US WITH COURAGE IN AN INCREASINGLY HOSTILE SOCIETY

Temptations, addictions, and distractions pull us down, discourage and confuse us. We swim in a culture highly influenced by our enemy, whose greatest goal is to blind us to what's most important—what's first. From scrolling endlessly on our smartphones, allowing FOMO (fear of missing out) to set our schedules, or getting lost in the stories of the latest celebrity or infamous scoundrel, we can look like little tin soldiers wound up to march in circles to the beat of someone who wants to destroy us. To shift our priorities and give us the strength to choose the best, we need a new awakening to the supremacy and beauty of our Savior, what he's done for us, and how to place him on the central pedestal of our lives. The Holy Spirit designed Hebrews to clear the fog from our eyes and infuse us with courage to live well in a hostile culture.

TO DISCOVER THE SPLENDID CONNECTIONS BETWEEN THE OLD AND NEW TESTAMENTS CONCERNING THE PERSON AND WORK OF CHRIST

Swindoll writes,

> As we begin to dive in, we'll soon discover that numerous ancient springs from the Old Testament contribute to its fresh message to God's people. Rich in history, vibrant in imagery, and eloquent in style, the book of Hebrews has the words to refresh our minds and cleanse our souls.[1]

Hebrews teaches us how to understand the Old Testament in proper relationship to Jesus. However, the many quotes from the Old Testament and references to the priesthood, the sacrificial system, and other unfamiliar Old Testament practices and events make the study of Hebrews intimidating to many Christians. But it's worth the work! We will discover that each of these Old Testament references in Hebrews beautifully foreshadows who Jesus is and what he's done for us.

Don't worry if you aren't yet familiar with many of these concepts— we'll provide notes to acquaint you with all you need to know to make these meaningful connections, enriching your faith and strengthening your perseverance. These connections display the splendor of our Savior, giving us compelling reasons to elevate him to his rightful place in our lives: first.

TO ANSWER THOSE "DECONSTRUCTING" THEIR FAITH

In the twentieth century, labeling yourself a "Christian" carried certain advantages. For example, if you ran for the school board or county commissioner, this brand communicated that you were likely a more honest person than someone who did not follow Jesus. If you sold cars, people trusted that you were more likely to offer them an honest deal. If you were looking for a spouse, a Christian would more likely be devoted to family. Undoubtedly, some people used this label to their own advantage, discrediting the name of Jesus and causing later generations to charge that the church is full of hypocrites.

Today, however, in the post-Christian twenty-first century, claiming to follow Christ can result in losing social clout, being overlooked for a job promotion, or experiencing family scoffing and even rejection. As a result, most people who claim to be Christians are usually the "real deal." If trends continue, American believers will probably suffer heightened prejudice and persecution in the future, like many Christians around the world are today.

Amid this changing cultural landscape, we see young people raised in Christian homes falling away from the faith in greater numbers than in the past. Typically, as they venture into adulthood, some experiment with other faiths and philosophies in their process to "own" their faith. This tendency is exacerbated because following Christ comes with greater costs. These young people are asking reasonable questions about whether or not their parents' faith is worth the risk.

And when costs are high, weaker believers are in greater danger of drifting away or asking whether they made the correct decision to follow Jesus. These are natural consequences in response to the changing times, and committed Christians need to take those people's concerns seriously. Instead of wringing our hands, let's walk with these strugglers and help them understand that the Christian faith is true. Jesus can stand up to their scrutiny. Consider inviting doubters to join you in this study. Hebrews was written to answer their valid questions and to ensure people that Christ alone is worthy of first place in all our lives.

THE WORLD OF THE HEBREWS

At the tender age of thirteen, my (Rebecca's) parents dropped a bomb on my younger sisters and me. My father had received a promotion, so we had two months to pack our rooms, say our goodbyes, and move from Overland Park, Kansas, to Shoreview, Minnesota.

Denial. Anger. Bargaining. Depression.

We cycled through the stages of grief, finally landing on grim acceptance.

My mother tried to soften the sting in the form of coveted Guess Jean overalls, retailing for $89.99. All the cool girls had them. And to a kid who'd only ever worn Kmart sneakers (minus the blue "Keds" label), they were indeed a prize. I supposed I could hold my head high at my new school in a pair of Guess Jean overalls.

And I did just that. With my hair hot-rolled and teased to formidable heights, I strode into my first class. A furtive glance around the room filled me with pride. *No one else has them.* Surely, they'd want to be my friend.

After the teacher introduced me to the class, a voice from the back called, "Hey, country girl! You're not in Kansas anymore. Why are you dressed for the farm?" Mortified, I slid down in my seat and tried to become invisible.

A chasm separated me from my classmates. Sure, we were from the same country and spoke the same language, but our cultures were as different as night and day. Once I learned the acceptable brands and appropriate vernacular, I fit in just fine.

Stepping into the world of the Bible requires an even greater assimilation process. You see, the Bible was written *for* us but not *to* us. God has miraculously preserved the ancient texts we call the Scriptures, but long before we beheld the leather-bound sacred words printed on gold-embossed pages, real people received them as inspired letters—penned by real people on papyrus scrolls, addressing real-life situations. To grasp what Hebrews means for us, we must first ask what Hebrews meant to them, the letter's original audience. We must enter their world, acquaint ourselves with their political system, and decipher their religious practices. Who were these people? Where did they live? How did they interact with each other? When we understand the context of the Scriptures, we draw out their deepest treasures.

FOCUS ON THE BIG STORY IN HEBREWS

Approximately four decades ago, my great-aunt Lucy introduced me (Rebecca) to the Chronicles of Narnia. I remember that Christmas well. I tore the bright paper off a slim package to find *The Lion, the Witch and the Wardrobe* by C. S. Lewis.

Great-Aunt Lucy knew I could lose myself in a book for hours, immersed in a distant world, and she chose the novel because she and the main character shared a name. By Christmas night, I had traveled through the wardrobe, met the lion, fought the witch, and watched Aslan breathe life into cold, gray statues. It wasn't until several years later, when I received the complete set of books, that I realized *The Lion, the Witch and the Wardrobe* was a small story set inside a larger narrative, and that Lucy wasn't the main character—Aslan was. As I devoured the series, I marveled at how much more I enjoyed these books in the context of the larger story.

Many believers handle the Bible the way I treated the Narnia collection. If we pull isolated verses from here or there, we tend to read the Bible with little understanding of the big picture. We place the wrong characters (or even ourselves) at the story's center and miss the point entirely. The results are tragic: David and Goliath become a lesson on giant slaying; Joseph shows us that we, too, can save nations when we submit to God's will. By making the story about us, we fail to see Jesus.

Every single book in the Bible points us to Christ. Each chapter contributes to God's epic of creation, fall, salvation, and redemption. And no book draws so deeply on our Old Testament heritage as the book of Hebrews.

Hebrews testifies to the supremacy of Christ. Outside of the Gospels, from the first stroke of the author's pen to the last, he (or she) offers the clearest picture of Jesus as the fulfillment of the Old Testament. In Christ we find the perfect priest, the perfect sacrifice, and the perfect intercessor. Hebrews pulls back the veil to reveal the majesty, supremacy, and ultimacy of Jesus the Messiah. And the richest treasures of the world pale in comparison to his glory.

We hope you're excited to move forward and discover how to ensure you never settle for second best!

THE AUTHOR OF HEBREWS

Many have attempted to solve the puzzle of the letter's authorship, but Origen, an early church father from the late second to early third century, said it best: "Who wrote the epistle, in truth, God knows."[2] The letter was widely circulated and (mostly) considered authoritative until it was formally recognized as canonical by Bishop Hilary of Poitiers in the fourth century.

Whoever the author was, he (or she) was steeped in both Greco-Roman culture and Judaism. He knew his way around the Scriptures, quoting and expounding on the Old Testament forty-two times. The letter contains the most artfully crafted Greek in the entire Bible, suggesting that the author received formal training in Roman rhetoric. This mysterious individual wrote the book for two primary purposes: to encourage his audience not to settle for second best and to remind them that they now had full access to God.

THE RECIPIENTS

Because the letter contains no initial greeting, we must search internally for clues about its original audience. In chapter 5 we see that the recipients had been Christians for some time, for the author admonished them that "by this time you ought to be teachers" (5:12). In chapter 2 we find that they were second-generation Christians who learned of Christ from "those who heard him" (2:3). This group of believers had also endured some persecution, as chapter 10 details. Because the author spent so much time drawing comparisons to the Levitical priesthood and sacrificial system, we know they were Jewish believers, most likely living near Rome.

We can assume the recipients were faltering in their faith because of the warning passages scattered throughout. We also know that once Nero ascended to the throne in AD 54, he deeply impacted the religious landscape. Christians, once only considered odd, were now regarded as threats.

THE ROMAN EMPIRE UNDER NERO

Scholars call Nero one of the most brutal dictators to have ever lived. With an upbringing worthy of *The Jerry Springer Show*, he rose to power at seventeen.[3] Nero's father loved strong drinks, a habit that frequently touched a lit match to his short fuse. He once killed a man who didn't drink enough for his liking, and another time he intentionally killed a young boy by driving over him in his chariot. But compared to Nero's mother, Agrippina the Younger, he was tame.

> Agrippina was characterized by vengeance, scandal, and political maneuvering. She made it her aim to instill these qualities in her only son, Nero. For Agrippina, personal relationships were valuable only if they enhanced her power and prestige. Nero was no exception in this regard. It was her constant ambition to rule the empire by proxy through her son. For this reason she groomed Nero for power and leveraged his political career to her own advantage.[4]

Nero had an unhealthy fixation on his mother, trying, unsuccessfully, to commit incest with her. When he failed, he forced one of his concubines to change her appearance to resemble his mother. In one shocking instance, he castrated two associates, dressed them as brides, married them in front of the crowds, and paraded them through the city.

The young emperor squandered money on gambling and lavish festivals. He resolved to build himself a golden palace and funded it by stealing gold, silver, and jewels from religious sites, along with property from the wealthy. In fact, historians say that Nero likely started the great fire of Rome in AD 64 to clear the streets and claim the land for his house of gold.

The fire ravaged Rome for six days. When the public grew suspicious, he blamed the Christians and ruthlessly sought "revenge." Anyone accused of following Christ could be arrested, thrown into the arena to be devoured by beasts, or publicly crucified. Victims lined the streets entering the city. Nero erected human torches to light his gardens by night—Christians nailed to crosses, covered in pitch, and set ablaze.

Many scholars date the letter to the Hebrews between AD 60 and 70, placing its recipients as prime targets for Nero's persecution. Judaism was socially acceptable and recognized by the Romans as a viable religion throughout the empire. One can easily understand why Jewish Christians might have been tempted to return to its familiar structures in the face of such oppression.

Claiming Christ as one's savior, a title reserved for the emperor, therefore came with a hefty price tag. In addition to official persecution from the Roman government, Christians who left Judaism faced expulsion from their families and synagogues. In a communal, honor-driven society, this brought deep shame in addition to the economic hardships and social ostracism that accompanied being part of an unsanctioned religion like Christianity. The author of Hebrews wants to assure these Christians that Christ is indeed better, despite the high cost of following him.

Better Because Jesus Outshines All Past Prophets and Spiritual Substitutes

Near the end of my (Sue's) senior year in college, my life crumbled and broke apart. My father was in the last stages of stomach cancer. My mother, always emotionally distant, bitter, and mean-spirited, withdrew and lashed out even more. A four-year romance deteriorated into chaos and confusion. Graduation loomed, and my mother's insistence that I study journalism now meant I had to seek employment in a field where I was not a fit. And I had loved the camaraderie of college life, but now my friends were preparing to fan out in a thousand different directions.

I knew God existed, and prayed often, but without a sure decision to follow him, a supportive spiritual family, or any biblical wisdom to guide me, I was an emotional and spiritual wreck. Many days a dark depression overwhelmed me, and when it did, I often retreated to our campus chapel. This chapel resembled a small European-style church, with rich wooden pews, velvet tapestries, stained glass windows, and a side garden punctuated with stepping stones, high walls of cascading vines, a rainbow of fragrant blossoms, and a bubbling fountain. Serene and silent, it was my private haven, a place of beauty to run to when I needed to escape from the distresses of the day.

One afternoon, when the burdens seemed particularly heavy, and my sorrows deeper than usual, I sat all afternoon in that chapel and wept, my heart and mind drowning in absolute despair. I remember praying, asking God to take my life because I didn't want to live anymore. As I sank deeper and deeper into a chasm of hopelessness, suddenly I heard a booming voice—I actually heard this voice audibly. The loud sound came from above me, but no one was visible, and the voice said just one word: *Wait*. Startled and shocked, I sprinted out of the chapel in terror. But as I've looked back, I know the voice was from God, maybe his angel, telling me that I was not alone, regardless of how I felt.

I seldom share this experience; I suppose I'm afraid people will think

OPTIONAL

Memorize Hebrews 1:1–3

In the past God spoke to our ancestors through the prophets at many times and in various ways, but in these last days he has spoken to us by his Son, whom he appointed heir of all things, and through whom also he made the universe. The Son is the radiance of God's glory and the exact representation of his being, sustaining all things by his powerful word.

I'm crazy. But, as we will see this week in our lesson, angels are real, and God can reveal himself to any of us however he chooses. Sometimes he speaks in a still, small voice. Sometimes it booms. Often he speaks through circumstances. However he speaks, God knows just what we need when we need it, and presents himself to us as best suits the situation.

Now that we have his Love Letter, the Bible, I don't think he speaks audibly or sends angels as often as he used to. But he can when he deems it helpful. In my case, I was desperate for a word of encouragement and strength, and in his mercy he sent that word. Four years later I heard the gospel, placed my faith in God the Father through Jesus, embraced a church community, and began the incredible ministry journey he planned for me.

I learned early in my Christian life that regardless of whether an angel spoke to me, the source behind that voice was God and the impetus for the message came from him. He alone is worthy of our worship, and we must be careful not to mix him up with angels, as we'll clearly see in our first Hebrews lesson.

CHRIST IS SUPERIOR TO ALL THE PROPHETS

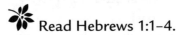 Read Hebrews 1:1–4.

1. How did God speak to his followers in the past? How does God speak to us now (vv. 1–2)? Make a list of reasons why this second way is so much superior to the first (vv. 2–3).

The old order [speaking through prophets] is associated with multiplicity and repetition; the new order is associated with the singular and unique Son.[1]
—Dana Harris

DIGGING DEEPER

In the first four verses, the author compares how God spoke to his people in the past—through his prophets—and now—through his Son. These Old Testament prophets include Abraham, Moses, Samuel, Elijah, Isaiah, Jeremiah, Daniel, and Hosea. Pick one and write an essay or create a chart comparing his ministry and message with that of Christ, God's only Son.

2. What was the Son's part in creating the universe and you? (See also Colossians 1:15–17 in the sidebar and Genesis 1:1, 26.)

The Son is the image of the invisible God, the firstborn over all creation. For in him all things were created: things in heaven and on earth, visible and invisible, whether thrones or powers or rulers or authorities; all things have been created through him and for him. He is before all things, and in him all things hold together.
—The apostle Paul (Colossians 1:15–17)

CHRIST IS SUPERIOR TO ANGELS AND ALL OTHER SPIRITUAL POWERS

Does it seem strange to you that the author begins his argument by emphasizing Christ's supremacy over angels? This choice may signal that the letter's first recipients were allowing their faith to be contaminated by false doctrines concerning angels. Even today people are attracted to similar forms of spiritualism.

The Son is not only the active agent of creation, but he is also active in the preservation of creation. . . . If the Son ever ceased to will the universe to remain, then the universe would cease to exist. The power to create is also the power to preserve, the power to control, and the power to bring to an end. Hebrews tells us the Son possesses this kind of power.[2]
—Albert Mohler Jr.

The Jewish Virtual Library reports that during their exile in Babylon centuries earlier, Jews became familiar with Babylonian myths that taught about sexual unions of their gods with humans. Some attempted to harmonize these myths with their Jewish faith, mixing Judaism with pagan legends. But in order not to contradict their "One God" doctrine, they taught that these strange offspring were angels.[3]

Similar superstitions persist today, such as in the popular musical *Fiddler on the Roof*. My (Sue's) Jewish friend of many years exhibited similar superstitions by shushing me and spitting "pu pu pu" whenever I suggested good outcomes, as if verbalizing them would encourage evil spirits to spoil the blessing.

Just like our first-century Jewish-Christian brothers and sisters, we can mix our faith with impure beliefs and practices that distort the supremacy of Christ in our lives. A healthy interest in angels is fine, but we must not give them undue honor or power, nor should we invoke the names of angels when we pray. Almost all false religions and cults began with a man or woman claiming a new revelation, usually from an angel, that contradicts orthodox Christianity.

For example, in the 1970s and '80s, the new age movement became a significant spiritual phenomenon that altered the spiritual climate of the Western world. Though its popularity had waned by the late 1980s, it left behind a plethora of pagan religious practices that continue to influence people today. Many new age psychics, known as channels, claimed they contacted angels or other supernatural beings, either in a trance or consciously, who communicated new spiritual truths.

More than one-fifth of adults in the West give credence to astrology. . . . Three to five million Americans identified themselves as New Agers or as accepting the beliefs and practices of the New Age movement in the late 1980s. The continuing presence of New Age thought in the post–New Age era is evident in the number of New Age bookstores, periodicals, and organizations that continued to be found in nearly every urban centre.[4]

N. T. Wright cautions us against becoming enamored with "shiny" spiritual additions to Christianity:

Not many readers today, perhaps, will be tempted to abandon Christianity in favour of some form of Judaism—though it is important for us to understand why that was such an obvious pressure in the early days. But many today, including many in the churches, seem dissatisfied with what they have, and are eager to expand their spiritual horizons (as they might see it) to include angels, saints and other interesting distractions.[5]

3. What do you know about angels? Do you find them fascinating? Strange? Scary? What role do they play in your life?

For those who choke too easily on God and his rules, theologians observe, angels are the handy compromise, all fluff and meringue, kind, nonjudgmental. And they are available to everyone, like aspirin.[6]
—Nancy Gibbs

4. Have you ever dabbled or been tempted to dabble in astrology, new age meditation, the healing power of crystals, or other supernatural practices? If so, why, and what did you learn?

5. Has an acquaintance or loved one been drawn into magic or the occult, or attempted to mix it with their Christian faith? If so, how did it impact their relationship with Jesus?

6. While many of us may not be tempted to worship angels, we can easily worship human leaders, subtly elevating them above the Lord. How easily do you idolize admired pastors, teachers, or politicians, believe everything an Instagram influencer or podcast adviser says, or subscribe to secular self-help books that claim you are good enough without God? Is this a temptation for you? Why or why not? Specifically, how can you keep Christ first in your life?

In 1 Corinthians, Paul writes to the Corinthian church, correcting them for their many unhealthy practices. He begins by addressing their obsessions, favoritism, and worship of human leaders above Christ. They had split into four factions, and quarreled based upon the teacher they identified with the most—Paul, Apollos, Peter, or Christ (1 Corinthians 1:12). If we aren't careful, we may find we aren't too different from these early believers.

✽ Read Hebrews 1:5–14.

Nowhere else in the Bible do we glean as much truth and insight into the nature and ministry of angels in one place. Here we observe seven quotations from the Old Testament revealing the difference between Christ and angels.

7. These seven Old Testament quotations begin by asking a question. What is the question, and what is its answer (v. 5)?

Angels, angels, everywhere! Modern descriptions of these celestial beings are plentiful: "visions," "kind people in disguise," "balls of whirling energy," "thoughts," "vivid dreams," "lights," "rainbows," "animals" and even "invisible hands." No wonder Christians have difficulty distinguishing modern-day angels from the kind they find in Scripture! What in heaven's name is happening?[7]
—Mary Drahos

8. From verse 6, name one of the primary privileges and responsibilities of angels.

9. In verse 7 the author quotes Psalm 104:4, a psalm praising God for his magnificent creation—"He makes winds his messengers, flames of fire his servants." What do you learn about the nature of angels from this verse?

Now God the Father proudly tells us about his Son and his future kingdom (1:8–12).

10. In verses 8 and 9, the author quotes part of a messianic psalm (45:6–7) that speaks of the second coming of Christ to set up his millennial kingdom on earth. In the first line of the quote, instead of "Son," what does God the Father call Jesus? Why is this important?

11. How long will King Jesus reign (Revelation 20:4–5)? What does he hold in his hand that reveals the character of his millennial kingdom (Hebrews 1:8)?

12. Read Isaiah 11:1–9 for more insight into your future home. What do you learn about the King's justice and the radical transformation of the earth? How do you feel as you absorb these marvelous truths? (For a more thorough understanding of your eternal future home, study *Isaiah: Discovering Assurance Through Prophecies About Your Mighty King,* another Discover Together Bible study by Sue Edwards.)

13. What position has God the Father given to God the Son and why? What primary emotion does the Son now exhibit as a result? (Hebrews 1:9)

DIGGING DEEPER

Study Philippians 2:5–11, which describes what theologians call Christ's kenosis, or "emptying." How does this beautiful passage complement this Hebrews lesson?

14. As you become more Christlike, would people say that you exhibit the "oil of joy" in your attitude and actions? Why or why not? Why is exhibiting joy so compelling in a believer's life? How might a sour spirit hinder our witness for the Son?

As powerful creations of God, angels conduct various services for the Lord. They carry His messages and perform His will among us—warning, protecting, helping, and rescuing. . . . They aren't a pantheon of "mini-gods" worthy of veneration; they are God's servants who, like us, render worship to Him alone (Rev. 5:13).[8]
—Charles Swindoll

Now the Father speaks to his Son (1:10–13).

15. What else do we learn about the Son that clearly shows he is superior to angels (v. 10)?

16. What will the Son do to begin the process of inaugurating the millennial kingdom and the new heaven and new earth (vv. 11–12)?

17. In addition, what does God the Father reveal will happen when King Jesus ushers in his millennial kingdom (v. 13)?

Nor are they [angels] cosmic go-betweens who pass messages for us from earth to heaven. Rather, they carry God's messages from heaven to earth. But as remarkable as angels are, their blazing light dims in the glorious blast of pure radiance that is the Son of God. Without denigrating the vital role of angels in the service of God, the writer of Hebrews puts them in their place in comparison with the person and the work of the Son.[9]
—Charles Swindoll

18. The author of Hebrews ends this section with a final question in verse 14. What does this question tell us about another primary task of angels?

BIG RED WARNING FLAG ONE
WAKE UP! PAY ATTENTION!

Throughout Hebrews the author pauses five times to wave a big red warning flag! He knows the temptations, challenges, and obstacles that await people living in a fallen world. Like a loving parent, he desperately wants to protect us from painful consequences that surely await us if we are not diligent, intentional, and attentive to what's going on around us. He shouts to us, "Avoid these pitfalls!" As I (Sue) used to say to my children, "I love you too much not to alert you to this danger."

 Read Hebrews 2:1–4.

19. What will happen if we don't heed God's instructions and tough-love warnings (v. 1)?

20. What do you think it means to "drift" in your spiritual life? Has this happened to you? Are you experiencing a time of drifting now? If so, can you discern why and how you might change course?

Verses 2 and 3 communicate a contrast. The "message spoken through angels" concerns the Old Testament law of Moses (Acts 7:53; Galatians 3:19) and its penalties for the nation of Israel when they disobeyed its commands. The "great salvation" (NLT) refers to our amazing redemption through Christ alone, by grace alone because of what he did for each of us personally on the cross when he shed his blood to atone for our sin.

21. Why is God's salvation "great" in your life? What difference has it truly made?

This is a warning many Christians need, perhaps especially those who have grown up in a Christian family or as part of a regular church community. It's all too easy to suppose that we can take the pressure off, and allow other people to do the praying, the thinking, the serious business; we'll go along for the ride, we'll stop putting so much effort into it, we'll go with the flow. The problem is that if we haven't got our own motor running, and our own hand on our own tiller, we may drift further and further away without realizing it.[10]
—N. T. Wright

The warning in Hebrews 2 is the danger of "drifting away." This leads to a forfeiture of blessings both now and in the future. This "drifting away" does not affect salvation, only rewards.[11]
—Stephen Kim

Believers cannot expect to escape just judgment for our neglect of the great salvation that is ours in Christ. For Christians, consequences of apathy and lukewarmness are reaped in this lifetime and at the judgment seat of Christ [2 Corinthians 5:10].[12]
—Irving Jensen

You see, God is either the God of perfect grace . . . or he is not God. Grace forgets. Period. He who is perfect love cannot hold grudges. If he does, then he isn't perfect love. And if he isn't perfect love, you might as well put this book down and go fishing, because both of us are chasing fairy tales.[13]
—Max Lucado

22. Verses 3 and 4 reveal more about this great salvation:

> How shall we escape if we ignore so great a salvation? This salvation, which was first announced by the Lord, was confirmed to us by those who heard him. God also testified to it by signs, wonders and various miracles, and by gifts of the Holy Spirit distributed according to his will.

Who first announced that this great salvation had come?

Who confirmed it? What did he say? (Mark 1:1–4, 14–15)

Who also confirmed it is true (Luke 1:1–4)?

What else confirmed this great salvation (Mark 1:32–34)?

How might gifts of the Holy Spirit (Ephesians 4:7, 11) confirm this great salvation is true? If you have experienced this confirmation in your own life, share it with the group.

23. Summarize what you learned in this lesson related to the following:

- the superiority of the Son over angels and any other form of "religion"

- the characteristics and ministry of angels

- the person and ministry of the Son

- how to make sure you aren't settling for second best in your life

THE MINISTRY OF ANGELS

Word spread quickly through my (Sue's) neighborhood after the accident. A dearly loved woman, known for her Bible teaching, typically jogged up and down our streets before dawn. That particular morning, after a night of partying, an intoxicated teen raced his car up and down our subdivision blocks, showing off his lack of mufflers.

No one actually witnessed the accident, and the teen fled the scene. Minutes later a neighbor heading to work spotted the woman's limp body in the street. Kneeling next to her, cradling her in his arms, was a stranger. He spoke to her in whispers as she gently passed into the presence of her Savior. No one knew where he came from, and he was gone before the police arrived. But those of us who know the sweet depths of our Lord's love were comforted by the witness accounts.

Angels are real! They are mentioned seventeen times in the New Testament and seventeen times in the Old Testament. However, we are not to worship them. Their power comes from God and is limited by God. They are finite, created spirit beings and, while normally invisible, they are able to appear as God desires.

The primary ministry of angels is to worship God, which leads them to serve God, mainly as his messengers. They deliver comfort and often protect his people from others, both spiritual and human.

God used angels to destroy Sodom and Gomorrah and to bring the plagues to Egypt. They will be the executors of God's judgments during the great tribulation. They seem to be present at the beginning of new eras and great events, such as the giving of the law at Mount Sinai, and Jesus's birth, resurrection, ascension, and return.

They guide, provide, strengthen, and encourage, but they are not the Holy Spirit. They are external; he is internal. They minister for us; he ministers in us. In the millennial kingdom and the new heaven and the new earth, we will rule over angels with Jesus. Won't that be exciting!

All these truths about angels are supported by biblical passages, and if you'd like to learn more, study C. Fred Dickason's book *Angels: Elect & Evil.*

Better Because He Alone Knows You By Heart

Some people struggle to understand why God needed to become human to reach us. I (Sue) will never forget Paul Harvey's explanation when he told a related story on ABC Radio, Christmas Eve, 2004. It went something like this:

A skeptical farmer told his family to go to the Christmas Eve service without him. He explained, "I just can't buy all this nonsense about God coming to earth as a baby." He grieved over the decision, but he was tired of being a hypocrite.

As he sat by the fire brooding and listening to the blizzard forecast, he was startled by a loud thud on the window, then another, and then another. He dashed to the window to see three tiny birds stunned and writhing in the snow. As the winds picked up, rattling the windows, he noticed the rest of the flock of petite birds huddled together on the fence outside. Suddenly he thought, *I'll coax them into the warm barn.*

He donned his parka, hat, and gloves and sloshed to the barn. He lodged open the double doors, turned on the lights, and waited. Nothing. The birds continued to sit on the fence, shivering.

He dashed back to the kitchen for some day-old breadcrumbs and spread them from the fence to the barn, hoping they would follow. Nothing.

He tried to catch them, but they flew away every time he came close. He tried shooing them in the direction of the barn, but they scattered and then returned to the fence.

Finally, he admitted to himself that all his efforts were hopeless—regardless of what he did, they were terrified of him. Suddenly he realized that to these helpless little birds, he must have seemed like a frightening giant.

Then he thought, *My only option would be to become a bird myself. Then I could show them the way to safety. Then I could speak their language. They would trust me and realize that I don't want to harm them. I want to help them. Then they could understand my true desire to rescue them. If I was one of them, then they would follow me.*

And then it hit him—and he dropped to his knees in the snow!

Imagine—God became human! It would be like us becoming a

OPTIONAL

Memorize: Hebrews 4:15–16

For we do not have a high priest who is unable to empathize with our weaknesses, but we have one who has been tempted in every way, just as we are—yet he did not sin. Let us then approach God's throne of grace with confidence, so that we may receive mercy and find grace to help us in our time of need.

My (Sue's) seminary professor Dwight Pentecost used to pepper his teaching with the word *selah* (pronounced see-lah), meaning "stop and intentionally reflect on what you've just heard before moving forward." A reflective pause. This practice will enrich your understanding of God's magnificent Word as you slow down and contemplate the truths before you and how to apply them to your life.

roach—small, dirty, and vulnerable. But he came to earth out of unfathomable love for you and me—so we would know that he knows what it's like to be one of us. Let that reality sink in as you savor the beautiful words in this passage. *Selah.*

YOUR DIVINE BIG BROTHER EXPERIENCED DEATH FOR YOUR BENEFIT

 Read Hebrews 2:5–9.

Now the author moves from Jesus's superiority over angels to his relationship with us. In verse 5 he explains that angels, unlike men and women, were not given dominion to "fill the earth and subdue it [or rule] over the fish in the sea and the birds of the sky and every other living creature that moves on the ground" (Genesis 1:28). Angels will not rule and reign with Christ in the millennial kingdom. We will.

Since different versions of the Bible translate this passage a little differently, let's all work from the New English Translation Bible, known for its accuracy related to the original language:

> "What is man that you think of him or the son of man that you care for him?
>
> You made him lower than the angels for a little while.
>
> You crowned him with glory and honor.
>
> You put all things under his control."
>
> For when he put all things under his control, he left nothing outside of his control. At present we do not yet see all things under his control, but we see Jesus, who was made lower than the angels for a little while, now crowned with glory and honor because he suffered death, so that by God's grace he would experience death on behalf of everyone. (vv. 6–9)

"Son of man" is used in the Old Testament to refer both to humans in general and to the Messiah Jesus, so here we have to decide if "son of man" refers to a typical human being or to the ultimate human being, Jesus, whose favorite name for himself was "Son of Man." Since this part of the letter emphasizes Jesus's humanity, verses 6–8 are most likely talking about a typical human being before transitioning to talk about Jesus later. The writer begins by asking a question in verse 6, quoting Psalm 8, as he teaches us how incredibly valuable we are to God.

1. When did God the Father crown humans with glory and honor? When did he put all things under our control? (Genesis 1:26–28)

2. Why aren't people in control of what's going on in the world now (Genesis 3:23–24)?

3. The end of verse 8 informs us that "we do not *yet* see all things" (NASB, emphasis added) under our control, but the verse implies that one day we will. When will we regain the status we enjoyed in the garden of Eden (Colossians 3:23–24; Revelation 20:6)?

> Then death and Hades were thrown into the lake of fire. The lake of fire is the second death.
> —The apostle John
> (Revelation 20:14)

4. Who makes it possible for believers to rule and reign in the millennial kingdom and the new heaven and new earth? How? Specifically, what did he do for you? (Hebrews 2:9)

Read Isaiah 61.

When Jesus returns to earth a second time, he will come back as a conquering warrior to cleanse the earth of injustice and all the abuse committed through the ages, preparing the earth for his thousand-year kingdom.

5. How does Christ's future return comfort those who mourn and provide for those who grieve (Isaiah 61:2–3)?

For the Church has no beauty but what the Bride-groom gives her; he does not find, but makes her, lovely.³
—C. S. Lewis

6. How will Jesus dress those who love him? What will each piece of adornment replace? (v. 3)

To him who loves us and has freed us from our sins by his blood, and has made us to be a kingdom and priests to serve his God and Father—to him be glory and power for ever and ever! Amen.
—The apostle John (Revelation 1:5–6)

7. Isaiah uses a botanical analogy to describe Jesus's beloved at the end of Isaiah 61:3. What is the analogy and what does it communicate? What do you think of this new name?

8. What will be one of the service projects for believers in the millennial kingdom (v. 4)?

9. What will be the primary service of many believers in Jesus's millennial kingdom? Who will support your work and honor you for your service? (v. 6) How can you prepare now so you will be ready for that future role?

10. In ancient civilizations, the first son in the family received a double portion of his father's inheritance. How many believers are considered honored first sons in God's family, and what does it mean that each will receive a double portion (v. 7)?

11. Have you ever lived in a place where natural beauty flourishes? Where righteousness and justice thrive? If so, that's just a foretaste of the millennial kingdom. Isaiah 61:2–11 describes the beauty of our future home. What analogies picture the changes of a post-fall earth to an Eden-like earth where righteousness flourishes and Jesus oversees everything?

YOUR BIG BROTHER PIONEER

 Read Hebrews 2:10.

Verse 10 reads, "In bringing many sons and daughters to glory, it was fitting that God, for whom and through whom everything exists, should make the pioneer of their salvation perfect through what he suffered."

12. What comes to mind when you hear the term *pioneer*?

What sacrifices did Jesus make to lead God's children into an intimate, eternal relationship with God the Father?

DIGGING DEEPER

In one of his letters to the church in Corinth, Paul reveals another name, similar to "pioneer," related to what Christ did for us (see 1 Corinthians 15:20). What is that name, and what do you learn about this concept as it was used in the Old Testament sacrificial system and calendar?

YOUR GIGANTIC SACRED FAMILY

 Read Hebrews 2:11–15.

The Greek word in verses 11 and 12 is *adelphoi*, which refers to God's family, both men and women. In this context, this word is best translated "brothers and sisters."

13. How large is your nuclear family? What does it mean to you personally that you are part of an enormous spiritual family, both now and for eternity?

In Hebrews 2:12 and 13, the author attributes several Old Testament verses to Jesus (Psalm 22:22 and Isaiah 8:17–18). In these Jesus identifies with us in our humanity and speaks about his thirty-three years on earth.

14. What did Jesus say or do during his earthly ministry to identify with us that are revealed in the Old Testament passages below, quoted in Hebrews 2:12–13?

Psalm 22:22

Isaiah 8:17

Isaiah 8:18

15. By coming to earth as a human, what else did Jesus do for us? How? (Hebrews 2:14–15)

The rapture is an event described in 1 Thessalonians 4:13–18 and occurs in the end times.

The Rapture will happen in a moment; Jesus will return, collect all living believers from earth, and transport them alive to heaven.[6]
—Mark Hitchcock

Believers will wait in heaven for seven years while the tribulation takes place on earth. After the tribulation, believers will return with Jesus to the earth where Jesus sets up his millennial kingdom.

16. How often do you think about the reality that, unless Jesus raptures you first, your physical body is going to die? Describe how you feel as you move toward your final day of this life.

17. Hebrews declares we can be "free" of the devil's desire and power to make us slaves to the fear of death (v. 15). How did Jesus break that power? Have you experienced that freedom? Why or why not?

DIGGING DEEPER

Paul explains a number of truths as he compares our physical bodies now with our resurrected bodies that we will inhabit during the millennial kingdom and the new heaven and the new earth. Make a chart comparing these two different bodies and comment on your observations and related emotions (1 Corinthians 15:35–50).

18. Reflect on 1 Corinthians 15:54–58. How does God desire us to live in light of the reality of our physical death?

YOUR DIVINE BIG BROTHER—FULLY GOD AND FULLY HUMAN

 Read Hebrews 2:16–18.

19. Hebrews 2:17 provides one reason Jesus needed to be fully human in order to redeem us from our sins. What is that reason? (We'll delve deeper into this concept later in our study.)

20. Why is Jesus completely able to understand and help us in our temptations, trials, and struggles (v. 18)? What do you need him to understand about your life right now? What do you think he experienced that enables him to identify with your challenges? How might this insight help you ask for help and be ready to act on his direction?

> Christ became like us, living in this in-between time—enduring the hardships, sufferings, and even death common to all of us. He, too, felt abandoned by God, trusted in Him through suffering, and became a testimony in this fallen world. Without this identification, He couldn't have said, "I understand. I know what you're going through. I know how you feel."[7]
>
> —Charles Swindoll

It started at age thirteen. Two cousins snuck me (Rebecca) a plastic cup full to the brim of champagne. The alcohol accomplished what nothing else could, calming my racing thoughts and taking the edge off my constant undercurrent of worry.

I had no hope. Hailing from a long line of alcoholics (most found sobriety), I would later receive a diagnosis of severe generalized anxiety. Moving every three years didn't help. By the time I graduated high school, I had a social dependence on alcohol. When I received my bachelor's degree from the University of Kansas, I was certifiably addicted.

By God's grace, I put the bottle down for good in October 2009. I still, however, carried two decades of shame. As the Lord healed my heart, I began to share my story. I'll never forget what happened after a particular women's event where I spoke.

I had centered my message on the story of the prodigal son in Luke 15:11–32. I identified with the younger brother, and God's grace toward him moved me close to tears. I knew how it felt to tuck one's tail between one's legs and humbly ask for help. Several women approached me afterward to thank me for my transparency. We exchanged smiles and hugs, and I went on my way.

Two days later I was winding through the aisles of a Christian bookstore when I heard someone holler my name.

"Rebecca? Rebecca Carrell? Is that you?"

I turned around to see one of the women I'd met at the event. She grabbed my hands and, through tears, told me about her son. He was an alcoholic too, and she had been too ashamed to tell anyone. After twenty minutes we parted ways—she, armed with my counselor's phone number, and me, marveling afresh at the Lord's grace.

I had ministered to her, and it had nothing to do with how well I'd taught through the Scriptures, my knowledge of the Bible's context, or my insights into the original language. She connected to me through my suffering. My deep shame drew her to me.

So it is with you and Christ. You can run to him because *he knows*. No temptation will come your way that your Savior has not overcome. And because he suffered and overcame, he can minister to you in your darkest moments. Your sin is paid for. Your shame was crucified on the cross. And if you allow him, Jesus will take your pain and turn it into your greatest ministry touch point.

Better Because He Provides Real Spiritual Rest

As a teen, I (Sue) plastered my bedroom walls with posters of popular movie stars and rock musicians. Once I sent off for an autographed picture of my favorite swaggering, pompadoured, one-hit wonder, but by the time I'd ripped open the envelope six weeks later some other guitar-strumming, undulating rock and roller had replaced him in the top forty charts. Disappointed then but grateful now, my limited access to the star hindered my fascination with fame.

Today, in our technological era, girls and women of all ages have immediate access to celebrities and can choose to spend hours scrolling through social media, interacting with their favorites on a variety of sites. As a result, research studies reveal that celebrity worship is on the rise. Statistics tell us that an unhealthy fascination with actors, singers, athletes, politicians, and "influencers" easily leads to all kinds of challenges and mental health disorders: anxiety, depression, eating abnormalities, sensation seeking, identity confusion, harmful daydreaming, addictive tendencies, compulsive shopping, social dysfunction, cosmetic surgeries, poor interpersonal boundaries, loneliness, and a lack of meaningful personal relationships. In addition, women are more likely to be obsessed with superstars than men. Often this obsession with fame is an attempt to compensate for something the worshipper values but lacks.[1]

Thankfully, another study indicated that the more serious both men and women are about their faith, the less they tend to worship famous people. However, the study also suggested that many religious people apparently ignore the first commandment, "You shall have no other gods before me" (Exodus 20:3), or else don't apply it to their worship of celebrities.[2] Obviously, this temptation, with all its adverse side effects, remains a danger to all of us, just as it did for the Hebrew readers.

In Hebrews 3 the writer cautions his readers, converts from Judaism to Christianity, to lay down their hero worship of Old Testament superstars because someone far superior has come on the scene. You may not make Moses your idol like they did or plaster your walls with the latest film star's

OPTIONAL

Memorize Matthew 11:28–30

Come to me, all you who are weary and burdened, and I will give you rest. Take my yoke upon you and learn from me, for I am gentle and humble in heart, and you will find rest for your souls. For my yoke is easy and my burden is light.

In 3:1, the author of Hebrews gives Jesus a title we see given to him nowhere else—"apostle." *Apostle* comes from the Greek word *apostolos*, meaning "sent one." The author wants to communicate that Jesus was and is our heavenly ambassador sent on an urgent mission to rescue us.

poster like I did, but it's likely that at some point you'll be tempted to put something on a pedestal that doesn't belong there, and your emotional health will pay a price. Thankfully, this week's passage will take a buzz saw to that pedestal, if you let it, which will help you run hard after the best rest.

CHRIST OUTSHINES MOSES

 Read Hebrews 3:1–6.

1. Instead of focusing on other people, famous or otherwise, who alone deserves our constant focus (v. 1)? What do you think it means to "focus" on someone and not on others?

The audience of Hebrews, converted Jews, grew up idolizing Moses. Many memorized Deuteronomy 34:10–12: "Since then, no prophet has risen in Israel like Moses, whom the LORD knew face to face, who did all those signs and wonders the LORD sent him to do in Egypt—to Pharaoh and to all his officials and to his whole land. For no one has ever shown the mighty power or performed the awesome deeds that Moses did in the sight of all Israel."

It's understandable why these Jewish converts would tend to see Moses and Jesus as equals. And the frightening persecution they faced tempted them to leave Jesus behind and go back to Moses and Judaism—but the writer of Hebrews argues that would be a devastating decision. They would be giving up something so superior for something so inferior, and the consequences would be dire.

2. The author compares Christ with Moses using the metaphor of a house (vv. 2–6). Use this picture to explain why Jesus is superior to Moses and all others we are tempted to worship.

3. Who is God's house now (v. 6; 1 Peter 2:4–5; Ephesians 2:19–21)? What would this mean to former Jews who had been taught that God's dwelling place was the Jerusalem temple?

4. Are you holding on to a bias or tradition that you need to let go of? If so, what is it? Why are you struggling to change? What's at stake if you don't?

BIG RED WARNING FLAG TWO

DON'T HARDEN YOUR HEART AND LOSE YOUR PRECIOUS REWARDS.

HELPFUL OLD TESTAMENT BACKGROUND

The original audience of Hebrews grew up with a thorough knowledge of the Old Testament. However, some believers today haven't had that opportunity. If that's you, read this summary to understand the rest of this lesson.

Jewish History and the Consequences of a Hard Heart

The Israelites suffered brutal slavery in Egypt for four hundred years. God promised to rescue them and provide a land of their own, the promised land, a place flowing with milk and honey. God called Moses to oversee their release and lead them out of Egypt, through the Red Sea, and into the wilderness to escape Pharaoh and his army, who were bent on annihilating them.

As they made their way to Canaan, the promised land, God designed their time in the wilderness to strengthen their faith and develop intimate relationships with him. He kindly led them step by step with a cloud by day and fire by night, and he provided for all their physical and spiritual needs. He also provided guidance for healthy and righteous living. However, over and over and over they bellyached, complained, failed to listen, and rebelled, even threatening to kill Moses. They refused to trust God when they didn't get their way immediately, and many developed cold hearts toward God.

When they finally arrived at the outskirts of the promised land, Moses sent in twelve spies to check it out. They discovered that the Canaanites were a powerful, bloodthirsty people, committed to worshipping abominable pagan gods. When the spies returned, ten of them, overcome with fear and lack of faith, focused on the dangers of trying to inhabit the land, even though God had proven himself faithful. Only two trusted God and returned with a hearty "Let's go!"

With few exceptions, the congregation hardened their hearts and sided with the ten. Through the night, the Israelites wept, grumbled, and accused God of betraying them. They shook their fists and shouted, "If only we had died in Egypt! Or in this wilderness!" (Numbers 14:2).

Finally, God had enough. He granted their wish: "I have forgiven them," he said, but "not one of them will ever see the land I promised on oath to their ancestors. No one who has treated me with contempt will ever see it" (Numbers 14:20, 23). So the entire generation of rebellious Israelites wandered in the desert outside Canaan for forty years, when the trip should have only taken two weeks. Only their children, as well as Joshua and Caleb, entered and experienced God's promise of peace, rest, and prosperity in the promised land of milk and honey.

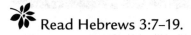 **Read Hebrews 3:7–19.**

5.   Specifically, who is warning the Israelites (and us) not to harden their hearts (vv. 7–8)?

The author begins by quoting Psalm 95:7–11, where he reviews what happened when the Israelites rebelled in the wilderness. He uses that incident to caution the original audience and us today so we don't follow in the Israelites' footsteps.

6. Since we live in these physical bodies, we are still burdened with a sin nature. As a result, we all sin from time to time. Have you ever sinned to the extent that you hardened your heart toward God? If so, when and why? What happened?

7. Although God ultimately forgave the rebellious Israelites, they still reaped a serious consequence. What was it (v. 11)? What consequences do Christians experience if they waste their lives by always going astray and not knowing his ways (v. 10)? Study the verses below carefully to discern your answer.

1 Corinthians 3:10–15

1 Corinthians 11:27–32

Hebrews 3:16–19

8. What is one of the most powerful ways we can protect ourselves from backsliding—that is, giving in to sin—so much that it results in hard-heartedness (vv. 12–13; 10:25; Colossians 3:16)?

9. Explain how involving yourself in a healthy church, various kinds of Christian gatherings, and investing in Christian friendships can help you maintain a strong spiritual walk and a soft heart toward God and others. If you can, share a specific time when one of these examples protected you from making a poor decision or responding sinfully.

DIGGING DEEPER

Analyze 1 Corinthians 3 to learn about God's strategy related to assurance of salvation and eternal rewards. Why do you think God devised both a Christian's assurance of salvation, based on the finished work of his Son, and the doctrine of eternal rewards, based on evaluating how believers live their lives?

So God gave them [the Israelites] time to think it over. He put the entire nation in time-out for nearly forty years. They walked in circles. They ate the same food every day. Life was an endless routine of the same rocks, lizards, and snakes. Victories were scarce. Progress was slow. They were saved but not strong. Redeemed but not released. . . . Four decades of tedium. Sounds miserable. It might sound familiar.[6]
—Max Lucado

CLEARING UP CONFUSION ABOUT THE MEANING OF HEBREWS 3:14

The King James Version of Hebrews 3:14 reads, "For we are made partakers of Christ, if we hold the beginning of our confidence stedfast unto the end."

The New International Version says, "We have come to share in Christ, if indeed we hold our original conviction firmly to the very end."

The New Living Translation reads, "For if we are faithful to the end, trusting God just as firmly as when we first believed, we will share in all that belongs to Christ."

What does it mean to be "partakers of Christ" or to "share in all that belongs to Christ"? At first reading, we might assume that we lose our salvation if we don't live an exemplary life. But how do we measure if we are good enough? And although we know consequences for deliberate, ongoing sin are real, none of us is capable of never messing up, and the Bible assures us that our entrance into his forever family isn't based on anything we do but on what Jesus did for us (Ephesians 2:8–10). How confusing!

The answer lies in the doctrine of rewards. Because Scripture really does promise that faithful believers will receive rewards in Jesus's future millennial kingdom, at the judgment seat of Christ, and those rewards determine how we will serve the King in his thousand-year kingdom.

So we make it our goal to please him. . . . For we must all appear before the judgment seat of Christ, so that each of us may receive what is due us for the things done while in the body, whether good or bad. (2 Corinthians 5:9–10)

New Testament scholar Paul Tanner states that "failure to do so [always obey] will not mean loss of salvation, but rather loss of reward (and possibly temporal judgment while on earth)."[7] Zane Hodges agrees: "A son who leaves home ceases to be an active partner in that home, though he does not thereby cease to be a son!"[8] F. F. Bruce addresses the importance of finishing well: "To begin well is good, but it is not enough; it is only those who stay the course and finish the race that have any hope of gaining the prize."[9] What is the prize? It's a marvelous future of rest and delightful service, sharing in "all that belongs to Christ" in his millennial kingdom.

Nevertheless, the Israelites who were not allowed to enter the land are a dire warning to each of us. Losing our inheritance in the millennial kingdom and the new heaven and the new earth will be personally catastrophic. To treat God with contempt, to assume upon his grace, and to be content with "fire insurance" will result in loss of rewards, loss of this marvelous inheritance, and possible regrettable consequences in this life (1 Corinthians 3:10–15). *Selah.*

10. Reread Hebrews 3:16–18. Have you been delivered from Egypt but are now, in some ways, perishing in the wilderness? What decisive action do you need to take to ensure that your life now and in the future will be all your heavenly Father desires? Seek the Lord, ask for help, and make a plan and stick to it.

There is no room here for the rather mealy-mouthed confession of faith one sometimes hears in the Western world ("some of us feel drawn to follow Jesus," implying that we might be wrong and that plenty of other people are just fine doing other things). Either you . . . can make sure and confident claims about it. Or you haven't really understood what Christianity is all about.[10]
—N. T. Wright

OUR PROMISED REST NOW AND IN CHRIST'S FUTURE MILLENNIAL KINGDOM

Read Hebrews 4:1–7.

11. Specifically, who is this passage written to? Who alone can enjoy the benefit of this kind of spiritual rest (v. 9)?

God offered the Israelites the promised land where they could live in peace, rest, and prosperity. But almost all refused to trust him, so they spent the rest of their lives wandering in the desert, miserable, anxious, and frustrated. The author of Hebrews draws parallels between these Israelites, his first-century audience, and us today. God pleads with us to trust him and follow his ways. He shows us how different our lives can be if we do. If you are weary of wandering in the desert, say yes to the invitation in Hebrews 4:1–13.

12. What is the continuing invitation in 4:1?

13. How can you forfeit the rest offered (vv. 1–2)?

14. When did God prepare this rest for his children (Hebrews 4:3–5; Genesis 2:2–3)?

15. How do we enter the rest God has provided for us (Hebrews 4:6)? In what areas are you experiencing his rest? In what areas do you still need to decide to go "in"?

What specifically is standing in your way of going in? Ask others to pray for you to overcome this obstacle.

16. When does God want you to take action (v. 7)? Why do you think your heavenly Father is so concerned that you act swiftly? What difference would it make in your life if you did?

 **Read Hebrews 4:8–11.**

After Moses died, Joshua led the next generation into the promised land, and the Israelites experienced rest, peace, and prosperity. They were under the Mosaic law, which was designed to guide the nation in living in right relationship with God and one another. Now that Christ has come, the audience of Hebrews—and *all* Christians—can experience an even greater rest: the rest that comes through Christ. Thus our author writes, "For if Joshua had given them rest, God would not have spoken later about another day" (v. 8).

17. What kind of rest is the author describing in verse 9? In what sense do we rest from our works, and why (Ephesians 2:6–9; Galatians 2:20–21; 6:14–15)?

Just as Moses could only take Israel so far, the Law can only take us so far. Just as Israel couldn't enter under Moses, we can't enter under the Law. Why? Because there's no rest under the Law. Israel had to be under Joshua like we must be under Jesus. Just as Israel turned back and forfeited the Promised Land, if we turn back from Jesus, we forfeit the spiritual rest He offers.[14]
—Scott LaPierre

DIGGING DEEPER

Contrast the Mosaic law and the salvation that comes through faith in Christ in Galatians 3:23–4:7. Apply what you learn to Hebrews 4:1–11.

Everyone ought to examine themselves before they eat of the bread and drink from the cup. For those who eat and drink without discerning the body of Christ eat and drink judgment on themselves. That is why many among you are weak and sick, and a number of you have fallen asleep [i.e., "died"].
—The apostle Paul
(1 Corinthians 11:28–30)

The author ends this section with another stern warning (Hebrews 4:11). The New International Version and other translations translate verse 11 this way: "Let us, therefore, make every effort to enter that rest, so that no one will *perish* by following their example of disobedience" (emphasis added). Tom Constable argues that "much confusion has resulted because Christians have interpreted 'rest' in this passage simply as reaching Canaan, in the case of the Israelites, and heaven, in the case of Christians."[15] We agree because using the word *perish* sounds like a believer loses their salvation through disobedience. The New English Translation Bible and others offer a less confusing and more accurate translation: "Thus we must make every effort to enter that rest, so that no one [who is a believer] *may fall* by following the same pattern of disobedience" (emphasis added).

18. What do you think the author means by the words "may fall"? What can happen if a believer continues to disregard God's directives and veers off the path, stalls, and then goes backward in their spiritual growth?

19. How does God want us to treat believers who have obviously "fallen"? What should be our ultimate goal? (1 Corinthians 5:1–5)

20. What believer do you know who's given in to the temptations of sin so much that now they are barely distinguishable from a nonbeliever? (No names, please.) What consequences have they reaped? What are they forfeiting in eternity?

> For the Son of Man is going to come in his Father's glory with his angels, and then he will reward each person according to what they have done.
> —The apostle Matthew (16:27)

21. If you have spent time attempting to help a believer who has fallen, share with the group what you learned to help them benefit from your experience.

THE DOCTRINE OF REWARDS—THE HOUND OF HEAVEN PURSUES TO RESCUE

One of the greatest sources of confusion and angst for Christians is what happens to believers who exhibit they are truly saved for part of their life and then fall away, or backslide. Some people say they were not saved to begin with, but in Matthew 7:1–2 Jesus said not to judge these matters. He was referring to the Pharisees when they took it upon themselves to determine who was in and who was out, and the same applies to us today.

Others have argued that those who "fall away" were believers at one time but lost their salvation because of disobedience. However, this reasoning goes against Scripture's repeated teaching that salvation is the work of Christ and, once accepted into God's forever family, permanent (Ephesians 2:4–10). No one who holds this view has been able to say just how much disobedience it takes to lose one's salvation.

Both of these perspectives turn Christianity into a faith just like every other man-made religion—one ultimately based on works. However, an in-depth understanding of the doctrine of rewards, as we've seen in this study, clears up the mystery. All who see their need for help, sincerely desire to change, and confess Christ as their Savior (based on his work on their behalf on the cross) become part of this forever family and are saved from hell permanently.

But God cannot be mocked—it matters how a Christian lives. Our obedience determines our eternal inheritance and how we will serve Jesus in his kingdom after the church age. Jesus will reveal how we did at the judgment seat of Christ, the bema seat (2 Corinthians 5:9–10).

In addition, God, as the hound of heaven, relentlessly pursues believers who fall away with a fervor designed to heap misery upon misery, to disrupt joy, and to block desires, all out of tough love designed to bring the fallen believer back to his senses. As we'll see later in our study, "It is a dreadful thing to fall into the hands of the living God" (Hebrews 10:31).

I (Sue) didn't come up with the term *hound of heaven*. Francis Thompson wrote a poem by that title to describe how God had pursued him. He was a believer who fell away and became an opium addict, living homeless on the streets of London for three years. He writes of his misguided love of self and of seeking affirmation in other people, lovers, children, and even nature. He ran from God in his early years, but God got his attention.

The hound can arrange severe mercies and harsh compassions to rescue lost Christians. Thompson's poem describes his rescue. Here are a few excerpts:

> I fled Him, down the nights and down the days;
> I fled Him, down the arches of the years;
> I fled Him, down the labyrinthine ways
> Of my own mind; and in the mist of tears
> I hid from Him . . .
> Adown Titanic glooms of chasmèd fears,
>   From those strong Feet that followed, followed after.
> But with unhurrying chase,
> And unperturbed pace,
> Deliberate speed, majestic instancy,
> They beat—and a Voice beat
> More instant than the Feet—
> "All things betray thee, who betrayest Me."
>
> . . . (For though I knew His love who followed,
> Yet was I sore adread

Lest having Him,
I must have naught beside). . . .

[God speaks] "Whom wilt thou find to love ignoble thee,
Save Me, save only Me?
All which I took from thee I did but take,
Not for thy harms.
But just that thou might'st seek it in My arms.
All which thy child's mistake
Fancies as lost, I have stored for thee at home:
Rise, clasp My hand, and come!
. . . Ah, fondest, blindest, weakest,
I am He Whom thou seekest!"[16]

The hound of heaven shadowed Francis Thompson. Just as he shadows all believers who fall away—God pursues them to rescue them, knowing the great inheritance and rewards that they forfeit for eternity unless they turn back.

Read the Bible in light of the doctrine of rewards and see these truths extinguish confusion and angst. They are designed to encourage us to serve God wholeheartedly, out of gratitude for his amazing grace—and to incentivize us to continue that joyful work throughout our lifetime and into the marvelous future God has planned for those who obey him. *Selah*.

Better Because He Never Disappoints Like Human Leaders

Just consider this amazing reality: You have access to Jesus, *your* great high priest who delights to be available to you 24/7! Unlike Old Testament priests or any religious or political leader today, he offers you pure, wise, and true direction whenever you enter through the curtain of your meeting place, a personal holy of holies, whether you sit on a stone by a river or connect in your closet at home. He doesn't shout slogans or demand you place a placard with his name on it in your yard or a bumper sticker on your car. He doesn't constantly ask for donations. He simply loves to spend time with you and walk with you.

Jesus was permanently elected by God the Father, his tenure will never end, and he won't ever go back on any of his promises. Misplaced loyalties are sure to disappoint because, after all, other leaders are only human. Reorient your allegiance to the only One truly trustworthy and give him your undivided devotion. Begin now by savoring the beautiful revelations about your great high priest in this lesson.

 Read Hebrews 4:12–13.

1. Verse 12 describes marvelous characteristics of the Bible with the words below. What do you think each word means related to the Scriptures? When have you experienced these attributes personally? How might they enhance your study of God's Word?

Alive

OPTIONAL

Memorize: Hebrews 4:12–13

For the word of God is alive and active. Sharper than any double-edged sword, it penetrates even to dividing soul and spirit, joints and marrow; it judges the thoughts and attitudes of the heart. Nothing in all creation is hidden from God's sight. Everything is uncovered and laid bare before the eyes of him to whom we must give account.

Jesus Christ . . . is the One who bears the blade of the inspired word of God—not as a sword to punish, but as a scalpel to heal. . . . We don't fight the Physician. We stop trying to diagnose our woes and selftreat our worries. We surrender our sins to Him. . . . Then we ask Him to do His work, trusting Him every bit as much as we would trust a skilled dentist or experienced surgeon. Yes, the heavenly Physician may cut where it hurts—especially as He treats the spiritual condition of a hard heart. But remember, He's not harming you; He's healing you.[1]
—Charles Swindoll

Active

Sharper than a double-edged sword

Judges the heart

2. The author reveals a sobering reality in verse 13. What is it, and when will this occur (2 Corinthians 5:10)? How is Hebrews 4:13 a strong incentive to seriously submit to Jesus's healing hand through a lifelong pursuit of loving and understanding the Bible?

3. What compels you to love, know, and apply God's Word? What hin-ders you? How can you make biblical literacy a priority in your life?

 Read Hebrews 4:14–16.

4. Because of Rome's brutal persecution, the Jewish Christians were tempted to abandon their Christian faith and go back to Judaism, which was officially sanctioned. Why does Hebrews advise against this (v. 14)?

5. Name some reasons why people today are tempted to walk away from their faith in Jesus. Why would it be foolish for you to abandon your loyalty to Christ?

> God never told us to be as holy as He is. That is impossible, and God knows it better than we do. He told us to be holy *because* He is holy, and there is a difference. Our holiness at best looks pathetic next to His. But we can grow in holiness, and He has made available to us everything we need to accomplish that.[4]
> —Richard Strauss

6. How is Jesus superior to all the high priests in the Old Testament (v. 15) and all the human leaders today and throughout history (Philippians 2:5–8; Colossians 1:15–20)?

7. As a result, what is our great and daily privilege (v. 16)? Fill in the blanks below to familiarize yourself with this exciting reality.

Let us then _____ God's throne of _____

with _____, so that we may receive _____

and find _____ to help us in our time of need.

8. In contrast, when could Old Testament believers enjoy this great privilege (Hebrews 9:6–7)?

9. As your great high priest, what is Jesus doing for you when you enter his most holy place (Romans 8:34)? Who joins him in this constant endeavor (vv. 26–27)? What are your thoughts and feelings as you consider these truths?

10. Stop right now and enter into his most holy place. Express the deep thoughts of your mind and the longings of your heart. What do you think the Son and the Spirit are now saying to the Father on your behalf?

A NEW EMPHASIS IN CHAPTERS 5–10

Thus far the author has offered compelling evidence that Christ is superior to angels and all other spiritual powers. He's superior to Moses and all other human leaders. He offers us an exceedingly better spiritual life, including peace and rest—far better than attempting to follow the Old Testament law.

The Jews and the disciples mistakenly believed that the Messiah would come to earth as a mighty king who would break Rome's iron rule and free them to enjoy political power and prosperity. As we experience cultural chaos, political turmoil, and racial division, we could easily yearn for a future military and political leader to do the same for us. But, in the first four chapters, Hebrews has refuted these misconceptions.

Now chapters 5–10 reveal that Christ is not only better in all the ways we've seen thus far, but he is also our future millennial king and our eternal great high priest, far greater than any earthly priest in the Old Testament or spiritual leader in the New Testament. We'll learn more about his excellence and sufficiency ahead.

 Read Hebrews 5:1–10.

We begin by comparing and contrasting the Aaronic and Melchizedek orders of the priesthood. God established the Aaronic priesthood to lead and serve in Israel's tabernacle and temple worship (Exodus 28:1). These were the qualifications of the Old Testament Aaronic high priest:

- He must be chosen from among men to represent men to God on their behalf.

- He must be able to sympathize with those he represents.

- He must be called and appointed by God to this divine service.

- He must be able to offer sacrifices for the sins of the people.

We will learn more about both priesthoods in lesson 5.

DIGGING DEEPER

To learn more about God's establishment of the Aaronic priesthood, study Exodus 28–29 and Numbers 17–18. List specific insights that you find interesting.

11. How does Christ meet and surpass the qualifications of an earthly, Old Testament Aaronic priest? Compare and contrast the old priesthood with the new. What kind of priest is Jesus (v. 10)?

Old Aaronic High Priest (5:1–4)	New Great High Priest (5:5–10)

BIG RED WARNING FLAG THREE

DON'T FALL AWAY AND STUNT YOUR SPIRITUAL GROWTH.

 Read Hebrews 5:11–6:3.

The author pauses, apparently in frustration, and rebukes his readers. Criticism isn't easy to hear, but it often provides an opportunity for reflection.

12. What is the author's first observation (v. 11)? What do his readers need (v. 12)? Is this ever true of you or someone you know? (No names, please.) If so, can you discern why?

13. What happens when a baby doesn't receive the nourishment they need to grow physically? What comparison does the author make to entice his readers to make a greater effort to grow up spiritually (vv. 12–14)?

> Only if we serve will we experience freedom. Only if we lose ourselves in loving will we find ourselves. Only if we die to our own self-centeredness will we begin to live.[8]
> —John Stott

14. What are you likely to gain by prioritizing the "solid food" of Bible study (v. 14)? How might that skill benefit you as you navigate life today?

> A man who professes an external law is like someone standing in the light of a lantern fixed to a post. It is light all round him, but there is nowhere further for him to walk. A man who professes the teaching of Christ is like a man carrying a lantern before him on a long, or not so long, pole: the light is in front of him, always lighting up fresh ground and always encouraging him to walk further.[9]
> —Philip Yancey

15. Where would you place yourself on the spiritual growth spectrum below? If you are disappointed in your progress, discern what's holding you back. If you are pleased with your growth, share with others what's helping you.

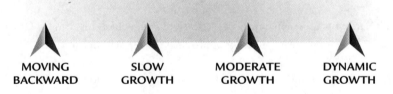

| MOVING BACKWARD | SLOW GROWTH | MODERATE GROWTH | DYNAMIC GROWTH |

One sad result of legalism is what it does to the legalist—either it cultivates a prideful, competitive, arrogant attitude that judges fellow believers and repels the outside world, or it fosters a sense of despair, of "I'll never make it," that too often leads to giving up and walking away.

16. What does the author advise in 6:1–3?

In Numbers 27:18–19, God tells Moses to lay hands on Joshua and commission him for service. This practice continues today when missionaries or ministers are sent forth by a congregation or group of leaders.

 Read Hebrews 6:4–12.

These verses have caused tremendous confusion for Christians through the ages. Note that the author writes using the first-person plural in verses 1–3 and 9–12. Examples include, "let *us* move beyond" and "God permitting, *we* will do so." But he switches to third person in verses 4–8: "It is impossible for *those*" and "to *their* loss." In the first instance he is talking to obedient believers, and in the second he is addressing believers who have fallen away.

Thus, the harshest rebuke isn't addressed to the author's readers but to a group of people who were still believers but had fallen away due to persecution. They had drifted so far that they had hardened their hearts and were probably beyond hope of repentance. The warning is for the author's readers, and us, not to follow in their footsteps. If we do, we risk terrible consequences in this life, possible premature death (1 Corinthians 11:27–32), and loss of rewards at the judgment seat of Christ.

Paul compares the obedient and disobedient Christian like this in 1 Corinthians 3:12–15:

If anyone builds on this foundation [Jesus Christ] using gold, silver, costly stones, wood, hay or straw, their work will be shown for what it is, because the Day [the bema seat of rewards] will bring it to light. It will be revealed with fire, and the fire will test the quality of each person's work. If what has been built survives, the builder will receive a reward. If it is burned up, the builder will suffer loss but yet will be saved—even though only as one escaping through the flames.

17. What phrases indicate that these people who have fallen away are legitimate believers (Hebrews 6:4–5)?

God has given us eternal life, and this life is in his Son. Whoever has the Son has life; whoever does not have the Son of God does not have life.
   —The apostle John
   (1 John 5:11–12)

18. What are the fallen believers doing (v. 6)? How do they contrast with those who live fruitful lives for Jesus (vv. 7–8)?

19. What does the author call his audience in verse 9? What will God never forget about them (v. 10)? What does God want them to continue to do, so their hope will be fully realized (v. 11)? What will they inherit by their good works (v. 12)?

Praise be to the God and Father of our Lord Jesus Christ! In his great mercy he has given us new birth into a living hope through the resurrection of Jesus Christ from the dead, and into an inheritance that can never perish, spoil or fade. This inheritance is kept in heaven for you, who through faith are shielded by God's power until the coming of the salvation that is ready to be revealed in the last time.
   —The apostle Peter
   (1 Peter 1:3–5)

 Read Hebrews 6:13–20.

THE CERTAINTY OF REWARDS PROMISED TO THE PATIENT AND FAITHFUL

The writer ended verse 12 exhorting these Jewish Christians not to become lazy, indifferent, or half-hearted in doing good (vv. 10–12) but instead to imitate one of their forefathers who waited patiently for God to fulfill his promised blessings.

In biblical times, when people wanted to seal the deal, they typically swore oaths by someone greater than themselves, invoking the name of someone with recognized greater integrity. This was their way of saying that the other person could count on the absolute certainty of the promise just made.

DIGGING DEEPER

Compare and reconcile the two passages below. How can both be true? Write a short essay explaining this reality.

1. Very truly I tell you, whoever hears my word and believes him who sent me has eternal life and will not be judged but has crossed over from death to life. (John 5:24)

2. For we must all appear before the judgment seat of Christ, so that each of us may receive what is due us for the things done while in the body, whether good or bad. (2 Corinthians 5:10)

20. How was Abraham an excellent example of patience, perseverance, and a recipient of God's promises (6:13–17; 11:8–12; Genesis 22:15–18)?

21. Remember that these Jewish believers were tempted to fall away from their faith due to extreme persecution. What did God desire to accomplish by revealing these two unchangeable elements—his oath and his promises (v. 18)?

22. What can you learn about the character of God from verse 18? Why is this quality important when you are struggling in difficult circumstances?

23. In verse 19 the author compares the Christian's hope to a metaphor related to a ship. What is it? What does the metaphor communicate?

24. This hope is also pictured as entering the holy of holies, the most sacred place in the temple, which the high priest alone could enter, and only once a year. Who secures this hope? What is he called? How long will he hold this position? (vv. 19–20)

> If Jesus were only a *really good* priest rather than a *perfect* priest . . . or if He were only an *above average* sacrifice for *most* sins rather than the *final* sacrifice for *all* sin, then we would have room to worry about just how secure our salvation really is. But because He is the perfect Priest, we can have confidence of our place of security in Him.[11]
> —Charles Swindoll

25. Are you ever tempted to walk away from your faith? If so, when? How might this lesson persuade you to keep persevering despite challenges and even setbacks?

IN DANGER OF DRIFTING?

One summer, our (Rebecca's) family of four flew to Ocean City, Maryland, for a family reunion and a week of fun on the beach. I mainly remember swarms of kids. Between me, my two sisters, and my two cousins, there were kids crawling out of every nook and cranny.

Here a kid, there a kid, everywhere a kid, kid.

By default, my adult sisters and I bore the task of child herding: Roll out of bed before the sun rose. Pour milk on cereal and wipe mashed bananas off chubby cheeks. Gulp down coffee. Slather on sunblock and coordinate single-file lines as we trudged to the beach. Text husbands to bring more coffee. Blow up beach balls. Wipe saltwater out of eyes. Race back up to the room for snacks. You get the picture.

On day three, my husband—sensing my exhaustion laced with frustration—took our kids back to the house to feed and nap them.

"You've got three hours," he said. "Do whatever you want."

I beelined for the foamy waves and spent the next forty-five minutes frolicking and reliving my own childhood. Finally, exhausted, I dragged myself out of the water and stretched out on the sand. Then I looked around.

Where was our green and blue beach umbrella? Where were the college kids who had set up camp next to us? Um, where was our *house*?

I jumped up and trekked what felt like half a mile until I found our crew. I had failed to notice that the current had gently nudged me due south while I swam.

The author of Hebrews warns of a different—but far more dangerous—kind of drift. Our culture drags us in a deadly direction unless we "pay the most careful attention" to the Word of God (Hebrews 2:1). The Greek construction of this verse suggests an ongoing, unceasing kind of attention. The storms of life can also sweep us away—the loss of a loved one, a grim prognosis, the death of a dream. Jesus offers "an anchor for the soul, firm and secure" to keep us from drifting (6:19).

Better Because He's Our One and Only Eternal Great High Priest

Who in the world was Melchizedek, and why does the author give so much space to this obscure Old Testament character? Most of us can't even pronounce his name (Mel-ki-ze-dek). Obviously, understanding him must be foundational to appreciating Jesus Christ's high priestly ministry in our personal lives, which must be instrumental to the formation of a deep, intimate connection with Jesus. This lesson unpacks what it means that Jesus is our great high priest in the order of Melchizedek. But we must dig down deep into Old Testament imagery of the law, the priesthood, the sacrificial system, and tabernacle and temple worship to uncover this buried treasure.

The original audience would have been thoroughly familiar with these concepts and likely even participated in these rituals for much of their lives. However, a lot of us are clueless about Old Testament practices, and we must persevere to discover the beautiful connections between the old and the new and what that means for us today. We assure you it will be worth the work because Isaiah promised that God's Word will never return void but will always accomplish his purposes in our lives (Isaiah 55:11). So get out your shovels, and let's get to work!

Reflect on this question: Do you believe you can approach God's throne directly and boldly, on your own, without another person serving as a mediator or go-between? If not, can you discern why? If so, when did you realize that through Jesus you can have a personal relationship with God all by yourself? What difference does this reality make in your life?

Let's begin by analyzing the only two Old Testament passages concerning Melchizedek.

 Read Psalm 110:4.

OPTIONAL

Memorize Hebrews 6:19–20

We have this hope as an anchor for the soul, firm and secure. It enters the inner sanctuary behind the curtain, where our forerunner, Jesus, has entered on our behalf. He has become a high priest forever, in the order of Melchizedek.

The book of Hebrews argues that Christ is the center and goal of Old Testament revelation—whether in direct messianic prophecies, prophetic anticipation, or even foreshadowing figures, as in the case of the mysterious Melchizedek. . . . With the coming of the Messiah, a whole new era has dawned, leaving the old system of Judaism in the rearview mirror.[1]
—Charles Swindoll

1. This psalm records the words of God the Father concerning his Son, the coming Messiah. What does God the Father announce about Jesus Christ in Psalm 110:4?

 Read Genesis 14:17–20.

Abram, later known as Abraham, the father of the Jewish people, was returning home, victorious in battle, when Melchizedek king of Salem (Jerusalem) came out to meet him. This event took place approximately one thousand years before David wrote Psalm 110—predating Moses, the Mosaic law, the first high priest (Aaron), and even the establishment of the Levitical priesthood and sacrificial system.

2. What did the king of Salem serve to Abram (Genesis 14:18)? What do these elements remind you of in the New Testament (Matthew 26:26–28)?

Scholars disagree on the identity of Melchizedek. Some think he was an angel, and others argue that he must be the preincarnate Christ. The prevailing view today is that he was a real, flesh-and-blood person, the high priest of the city of Jerusalem—someone, like Abraham, who worshipped the one true God and someone of outstanding character, as illustrated by his name. The author of Hebrews writes that he resembled the Son of God (7:3). The Greek word means "to make one thing resemble another thing." Thus, Melchizedek exhibited some striking similarities to our eternal great high priest, Jesus Christ. So we would call Melchizedek a "type of Christ." A type is a picture, symbol, pattern, or shadow of something in the Old Testament that obviously foreshadows something or is fulfilled in the New Testament.

3. What is unusual about this king who suddenly appears to Abram as a high priest of "God Most High"? What do Melchizedek and Abram have in common (Genesis 14:18)?

4. In Genesis 14:19–20, Melchizedek blessed Abram. Why is this significant?

5. How does Abram respond to this encounter (v. 20)? What does this tell you about Abram's assessment of this experience?

> Types are pictures, object lessons, by which God taught His people concerning His grace and saving power. The Mosaic system was a sort of kindergarten in which God's people were trained in Divine things, by which also they were led to look for better things to come. . . . God in the types of the last dispensation was teaching His children their letters. In this dispensation He is teaching them to put the letters together, and they find that the letters, arrange them as they will, spell Christ, and nothing but Christ.[2]
>
> —William Moorehead

Read Hebrews 7:1–3.

The writer of Hebrews tells us more about Melchizedek and the meaning of this strange encounter with Abram.

6. In the Bible, names often reveal character qualities. What does the name Melchizedek mean (v. 2)?

7. Fill in the blanks below (v. 3):

Without ____________________ or ________________________,

without ____________________, without ____________________

____,

resembling ________________, he remains ________________.

The scant historical record in Genesis 14:18–20 makes no mention of his [Melchizedek's] parentage, ancestry, progeny, birth, or death. He simply appeared as if out of nowhere. . . . Of course, as a mortal man, Melchizedek had been born and did die, but as a biblical figure, what Melchizedek was in the narrative [without recorded beginning or end], Christ is in His nature [without actual beginning or end]. . . . What Melchizedek was in the narrative, the Messiah is in His nature—Jesus is Priest and King, Righteousness and Peace incarnate, eternal in His deity, and ever able to serve as High Priest in heaven.[3]
—Charles Swindoll

What is unusual about this king (v. 3)?

 Read Hebrews 7:4–10.

Here the author contrasts the work of the Old Testament Aaronic priests, who were still offering sacrifices in the temple in Jerusalem at this time, with Jesus's priestly eternal sacrifice, symbolized by the priestly order of Melchizedek.

8. Who did God call as his first priests when he initiated the Old Testament sacrificial system in the tabernacle and later in the temple? They could only be chosen from one of the twelve Israelite tribes. Which one?

Centuries earlier, during his suffering, Job yearned for a mediator to plead his case to God, but no such person arose. Job stood alone before the Almighty. But we are blessed with a mediator—Jesus, our personal high priest.

What do you learn about this priesthood from the following passages?

Exodus 29:44–46

Numbers 3:1–3; 18:21

2 Chronicles 31:2

9. Why is Melchizedek greater than Abraham (vv. 4, 7)?

10. Why is Melchizedek greater than any of the Aaronic priests (vv. 5–10)?

※ Read Hebrews 7:11–28.

The author continues his argument that Jesus has negated the need for the Aaronic priesthood.

11. Now that we have a superior priest and priesthood, what else is no longer needed? Why? What is the better hope referred to? (vv. 12, 18–19)

12. How does Paul answer the question, "Why, then, was the law given?" How long was the law meant to last? (Galatians 3:19) Has this "seed" or "child" come? What does this mean about the law?

13. According to Romans 7:7–8, what does the law do? If you saw the sign below posted above a hole in a wall, what would you be tempted to do? If the sign wasn't there, what would you be likely to do?

14. What did Jesus do to the Mosaic law (Matthew 5:17)? When an expert in the law asked Jesus which commandment was the greatest, how did Jesus respond (22:37–38)? How do Jesus's words change your understanding of the law and our priorities as we live out our lives as believers?

Legalism means attempting to merit salvation by doing good works or obeying the law. This idea is contrary to all Christian doctrine.

15. Why do you think works–based righteousness entices so many people? Are you sometimes tempted to fall back into legalism rather than trust your all-sufficient great high priest for the power to live out his supernatural love? If so, can you discern why?

But the fruit of the Spirit is love, joy, peace, forbearance, kindness, goodness, faithfulness, gentleness and self- control. Against such things there is no law. Those who belong to Christ Jesus have crucified the flesh with its passions and desires. Since we live by the Spirit, let us keep in step with the Spirit.
    —The apostle Paul
    (Galatians 5:22–25)

16. According to Hebrews 7:13–16 and 23–28, what other differences exist between the Aaronic priests and Jesus, a priest in the order of Melchizedek? What is the point of verse 16?

17. What oath, or promise, makes Jesus—in the order of Melchizedek—far superior to the priests in the Old Testament (vv. 20–21)? Who made this promise?

18. Jesus's work on your behalf did not end after he endured crucifixion and was resurrected. What is he doing for you right now (v. 25)? What difference could this realization make as you walk through various circumstances in this fallen world?

The superiority of Jesus' high priesthood is clear from four facts: (1) Jesus' priesthood did not depend on His ancestors but on Himself alone, (2) Jesus lives forever and never dies, (3) Jesus is sinless and never needs to offer a sacrifice for His own sins, and (4) Jesus offered a perfect and adequate sacrifice.

In view of the superior order of priesthood that Melchizedek foreshadowed, and that Jesus Christ fulfilled, why would anyone want to go back to the old Aaronic order?[6]
—Thomas Constable

19. On the continuum below, how would you assess your intimacy with Jesus? Can you discern why? How might you move more toward a closer walk with your Savior?

Distant **Somewhat Distant** **Somewhat Close** **Usually Close** **Extremely Close**

JESUS IS THE GREAT HIGH PRIEST IN THE NEW HEAVENLY SANCTUARY

 Read Hebrews 8:1–5.

God designed the whole Mosaic system to be a huge object lesson, pointing forward to a system that would be better. Judaism was founded to prefigure Christianity, and even Israel's history was intended to guide Christ-followers today. Paul agrees when he writes, "These things happened to them as examples and were written down as warnings for us, on whom the culmination of the ages has come" (1 Corinthians 10:11).[7]

20. Instead of ministering in an earthly tabernacle or temple in Jerusalem, where does Jesus, our great high priest, minister (vv. 1–2)?

Just as a photograph of my family is merely a visual representation of my real, flesh-and-blood family, the earthly tabernacle and earthly priesthood are a representation of the real, heavenly tabernacle and heavenly priesthood.[8]
    —Charles Swindoll

21. Once a year, the Aaronic high priest offered a temporary sacrifice for his own sin and the sins of the people (v. 3). What does Jesus bring to sacrifice instead?

22. How were the earthly tabernacle and temple in the Old Testament similar to the sanctuary where Jesus now serves as our great high priest (v. 5)? How were they different?

Of all the furniture in the temple, one item that was not present was a chair or couch on which the priests could sit. This was because their work of offering sacrifice for sin was never finished. In contrast, because the sacrifice Christ offered was perfect and complete, when His work was finished, He sat down at the right hand of God. Not only does this vividly show us that His work is complete; it also shows that when His sacrifice is applied to our sins, that payment is complete and perfect. We cannot add to it, we cannot improve on it, and we cannot lose it.[9]
—Dwight Pentecost

JESUS IS THE GREAT HIGH PRIEST OF THE NEW COVENANT

 Read Hebrews 8:6–13.

23. According to verses 6 and 7, what is another reason Jesus's ministry is superior to the old system?

DIGGING DEEPER

Exodus 25–27 provides detailed instructions for the construction of the tabernacle. Since this edifice is a "shadow" of the heavenly place where Jesus now serves as our great high priest, what can you discern about the heavenly sanctuary from these verses?

24. Why did God need to establish a new covenant (vv. 8–12)? When did the old covenant disappear (v. 13)? How is this new covenant different from the old Mosaic covenant that includes the law? What's exciting and beautiful about this new covenant?

25. What do you think it means that God now writes his laws in your mind and on your heart (v. 10)? Do you experience this reality in your daily life? If so, how?

26. Verses 11 and 12 promise that we as believers will have access to some kind of internal knowledge or "teaching" that will guide us because our sin has been forgiven. How do you think the ideas presented in these two verses work together to provide us with the supernatural help we need to flourish in the world today?

THE POWER OF THE NEW COVENANT

by Brittany Mann

In C. S. Lewis's fifth installment of the Chronicles of Narnia, *The Voyage of the Dawn Treader*, young Lucy discovers a magic book full of spells. She's especially fascinated by a spell that promises to make her the most beautiful mortal in the world. Lucy has always coveted the beauty of her big sister, Susan. Now, in her mind's eye, she sees a vision of herself transformed into a dazzling beauty. Tempted, Lucy decides to say the spell, even though she knows it isn't wise. Just as she begins to utter the first words, Aslan's face appears bright on the page and growls. She quickly slams the book shut, avoiding a grave mistake.

Throughout the series, Aslan embodies Jesus Christ. He is both creator and sustainer of Narnia. Yet he is also personal to all those who believe in him. Lewis portrays Lucy's growing love and faith in Aslan. Her unwavering belief in him surpasses that of her siblings, allowing her to see him when others cannot. In the scene above, we see Aslan lovingly protect Lucy as she faces temptation and peril. He is not with her in body, but he is with her in spirit—in her very heart and mind.

In the same way, Christians under the superior new covenant experience Jesus and the Holy Spirit's supernatural protection and guidance. In Hebrews 8 the author reminds us that the law is no longer found as external written rules, but instead God says, "I will put my laws in their minds and write them on their hearts" (v. 10).

The Holy Spirit helps us put God's law of love into action by teaching us, convicting us, and spurring us on to good works. While Jesus is intervening for us in the heavenly sanctuary, the Holy Spirit increases our intimacy with him, purposefully making us more like him. Like the face of Aslan in the story, the Spirit supernaturally guides us and helps us take each wise step. He marks us as God's children, bringing to life the words of the prophet Jeremiah, "I will be their God, and they will be my people" (v. 10).

One day all will know him as we do. And for those of us in Christ, we can look expectantly to a grand future of true freedom from sin and serving with Jesus in his millennial kingdom and the new heaven and the new earth. This is the privilege of the believer and the power of the new covenant—and why it's so much better than the old. *Selah.*

Better Because We Possess Full Access to the Heavenly Sanctuary

Keep Out signs abound. Roadblocks protect us from dangerous hazards. Passwords guard against others accessing our phones, computers, and bank accounts. Try getting past the police tape caging a crime scene. In contrast, we need special means to gain access to particular places. Hotel room cards keep strangers from disturbing our privacy when we travel. We pay extra for backstage passes to meet a favorite entertainer. Prepaid tickets open the gate to special sporting or entertainment events.

But what about access to God? People have always desperately searched for ways to connect with God, hoping to find answers to the mysteries of the universe. Is God accessible? Paul Tautges asks,

> Is it inconsistent for the Bible to teach us that God "dwells in unapproachable light" . . . while at the same time exhort us to draw near to him? If God dwells in the white-hot light of his holiness, how can sinners like you and me ever hope to take even one baby step toward him? If God is so pure, so completely undefiled, so sharply separate from sin, how can we approach him? Indeed, it seems, he is unapproachable.[1]

Yes, God is unapproachable to those *without* the all-access pass that comes with putting one's faith in Christ as Savior. But if you have responded to Jesus's invitation to join his forever family, you have a 24/7 ticket into his heavenly sanctuary. God opens his arms to you perpetually and permanently in this sanctuary. The Bible foreshadowed this wondrous reality thousands of years ago when God gave Moses painstakingly exact instructions to build an earthly tabernacle that paralleled a heavenly sanctuary, where God waits to meet with you right now.

This lesson lays out fascinating comparisons and contrasts between the earthly and heavenly sanctuaries, the old and new covenants, and the different privileges of God's beloved children before and after Christ. Deep calls to deep, so find "God's Book, your nook, and [take] a long look."[2]

 Read Hebrews 9:1–5.

THE TEMPORARY EARTHLY SANCTUARIES—TABERNACLE AND TEMPLE

After the Israelites left Egypt and while they wandered in the desert, they carried a portable tentlike structure called the tabernacle. Whenever they stopped, the Levites would reassemble the different parts of the tabernacle, creating a temporary place of worship. God gave Moses detailed instructions on exactly how each part should look as well as how to perform ceremonies for the sacrificial system and services. Each specific direction symbolized a future truth that blesses believers today.

1. Below is a drawing of the earthly tabernacle, or sanctuary, where the Israelites carried out the regulations for worship under the Mosaic covenant. Indicate which parts are mentioned in Hebrews 9:1–5. What was contained in the ark of the covenant?

DIGGING DEEPER

For details on the creation and setup of the tabernacle, study Exodus 35–40. What parallels can you observe that relate to Christ's redemptive plan and the benefits for all who follow him?

Where was the altar of incense? According to Old Testament instructions, it was normally just outside the veil to the holy of holies, but according to the author of Hebrews, on the Day of Atonement it was located within the holy of holies. Was it inside or outside? Some scholars suggest that on the Day of Atonement, the high priest adjusted the veil of the holy of holies so that it temporarily wrapped around the altar of incense. The smoke would then fill the holy of holies during this most sacred ritual offering.

The Tabernacle

The Most Holy Place

Ark of the Covenant

Veil

Altar of Incense

Table of Shewbread

Candlestick

The Holy Place

Laver

Altar of Sacrifice

Outer Courtyard

Gate

Read Hebrews 9:6–10.

2. Specifically, where did the priests carry out their daily duties (v. 6)?

3. Verse 7 explains that the high priest would only enter the most holy place (the holy of holies) once a year, on the Day of Atonement. What did he take with him? What did he do there? Why?

Sin can be divided into three categories. Sins of commission are when we know what we are doing is wrong. Sins of omission are when we know what to do but don't do it. A third category is sins committed in ignorance (or unintentional sin). According to Hebrews 9:7, the high priest offered a sacrifice once a year in the most holy place for this third kind of sin . . . which leaves us wondering, What about the first two kinds of sin?

4. Observe verse 8 carefully by filling in the blanks below. What do you think verse 8 means?

The Holy Spirit was showing by this that the way into

the ____________________ had not yet been disclosed as long

as the __________________ was still functioning.

5. Verses 9 and 10 reveal that even the once-a-year blood sacrifice by the high priest in the most holy place (the holy of holies) was "not able to clear the conscience of the worshiper." Think of a time when you experienced a guilty conscience and share it with the group if you are comfortable. What do you think it means to "clear the conscience" of the worshipper?

6. A veil or curtain hung between the holy place and the most holy place. What do you think the Holy Spirit was attempting to teach Old Testament worshippers and us by designing the tabernacle with this veil blocking the holy of holies?

7. The Jerusalem temple was patterned after the tabernacle. What oc-curred immediately after Jesus died on the cross (Matthew 27:51–52)? What is the significance of the veil between the holy place and the most holy place tearing from top to bottom? What did this symbolize?

8. If these repetitive rituals performed by Old Testament priests couldn't actually cleanse the Israelites from sin, what might have been their purpose (Hebrews 9:8–10)?

9. Because the sacrificial system didn't actually cleanse the Israelites from sin, how did they get right with God (Genesis 15:4–6)? Since the foundation of the world, what has been the only way for someone to be accepted into God's forever family (Galatians 3:5–9)? What is the significance of this truth?

THE PERMANENT HEAVENLY SANCTUARY

 **Read Hebrews 9:11–14.**

10. How is the heavenly sanctuary different from the earthly one (v. 11)?

11. According to verse 12, where does our great high priest dwell now? How did he get there? What did he obtain as a result?

12. What did Christ do in the heavenly sanctuary that no one could ever accomplish in the earthly sanctuaries (vv. 13–14)? Why? What is Jesus's ultimate purpose for Christians? Are you living out that purpose? If so, how?

THE NEW COVENANT

 Read Hebrews 9:15–24.

We've just learned that Christ is our great high priest and that he continuously intercedes for his beloved children in his heavenly sanctuary. In addition, he has inaugurated the new covenant.

13. The Old Testament prophet Jeremiah announced the coming of the new covenant to Israel first. Why was the new covenant needed? What is new about it? (Jeremiah 31:31–34)

DIGGING DEEPER

Is Israel still God's chosen people? Study Romans 9–11 for insight and write an essay detailing God's affection and plan for the Jewish people.

14. Jesus also announced the new covenant to his disciples in the upper room the night before his crucifixion (Matthew 26:27–28). Describe what happened there. What incredible advantage do believers receive as a result (Hebrews 9:15)?

15. Paul describes the great contrast between the old and new covenants in 2 Corinthians 3:5–11. Make two lists: one describing the old covenant and one describing the new covenant. Why is the new covenant far more glorious?

Old Covenant	New Covenant

16. In verse 16 the author compares the new covenant to a will. What must happen before a will can go into effect? Why was a blood sacrifice needed for both covenants (Hebrews 9:16–24; Leviticus 17:11)?

Because sin is a horrible offense against a holy God, atonement for sin is costly. The costliest thing in God's creation is life. And an animal's life is in the blood (Lev. 17:11). Therefore, it necessarily follows that "without shedding of blood, there is no forgiveness" (Heb. 9:22).[10]
—Charles Swindoll

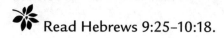

✳ **Read Hebrews 9:25–10:18.**

You are now invited beyond the veil, to delight in His presence. In response, your heart cries, "You will fill me with joy in your presence, with eternal pleasures at your right hand" (Psalm 16:11).[11]
—Jennifer Dean

17. What is the main difference between the Old Testament priests' offerings and the offering of our great high priest (9:25–10:18)?

18. Jesus came to earth the first time to establish the new covenant through his sacrifice on the cross. What will be his main mission when he returns to earth a second time (9:28)? What kind of "salvation" do you think the author alludes to here (1 Thessalonians 2:11–12; 5:9–10)?

The period of time right up to the coming of the Messiah . . . was simply the time of temporary arrangements (and the temporary arrangements included, confusingly, the entire tabernacle or Temple itself!). Don't make the mistake of thinking that this whole system, elaborate and well constructed though it is, is what God has in mind as the final scheme.[12]
—N. T. Wright

19. Contrast the posture of the Old Testament priests with our great high priest (Hebrews 10:11–12). What does this signify?

20. What marvelous benefits do believers obtain in the new covenant (vv. 10, 14, 16–17)? Do you live in the reality of these truths? If not, what difference would it make if you did?

21. Since the time Jesus initiated the new covenant through the cross, what has he been waiting for (v. 13)? (See also Psalm 110, where God the Father speaks to God the Son.) What do you think this means? How will your life be different once God the Father has made all creation the Son's footstool?

22. Do you ever struggle with the value of prayer? With how to pray? With what prayer actually means and accomplishes? Does your 24/7 access to Jesus, and the inner sanctuary in the heavenly sanctuary, change your thoughts about prayer? If so, in what way?

23. Because of the ministry of your great high priest, you have immediate
and direct access to God. What does that privilege mean to you? What
burdens do you need to bring to his throne of grace right now?

Lord, heighten my spiritual senses to
see that which is not visible
hear that which is not audible
sense that which is not tangible . . .

Teach me to sort through
the noises of this world to
hear and discern Your powerful,
wonderful, pure, precious voice.[16]

Better Because He Empowers Us to Persevere

The year I (Rebecca) graduated from high school in Colorado, my friend Becky and I resolved to check a box on our bucket list and signed up for the Georgetown to Idaho Springs Half Marathon. The course begins in Georgetown, Colorado (elevation eighty-five hundred feet above sea level), and winds its way down the mountain to finish in Idaho Springs (elevation seventy-five hundred feet). Each year, thousands of people stream in from all over the world with hopes of securing a PBT (personal best time).

We took our training seriously, even committing to a rigorous schedule when we traveled to Puerto Vallarta, Mexico, for our senior class trip. Each of the seven days we set our alarms, strapped on our shoes, and hit the hot Mexican pavement.

We persevered all summer. Every day we'd start out laughing and chatting but huff and puff the last few miles, collapsing into red-faced heaps at the end. By the time we hit race day, however, our training had paid off. We crossed the finish line a good ten minutes faster than we'd hoped.

Long-distance running requires endurance, a recurring theme in the last chapters of Hebrews. The author's audience likely suffered great persecution under Nero's reign (see introduction) and needed encouragement to "hold unswervingly to the hope" in Christ (Hebrews 10:23). Judaism, a religion accepted by the Roman Empire, presented Jewish Christians with a tempting offer: keep the Jewish God, deny Christ, and avoid oppression.

As Christianity curries less and less favor in our culture, we too might be tempted to quietly quit. But in the strongest terms, the author admonishes us that if we deny Christ, we have nowhere else to turn for salvation. But when we endure to the end, we will receive valuable rewards as we cross the finish line.

OPTIONAL:

Memorize Hebrews 12:1–3

Since we are surrounded by such a great cloud of witnesses, let us throw off everything that hinders and the sin that so easily entangles. And let us run with perseverance the race marked out for us, fixing our eyes on Jesus, the pioneer and perfector of faith. For the joy set before him he endured the cross, scorning its shame, and sat down at the right hand of the throne of God. Consider him who endured such opposition from sinners, so that you will not grow weary and lose heart.

PRESS ON IN YOUR FAITH

 Read Hebrews 10:19–25.

As we saw in lesson 6, Israel's high priest ventured into the most holy place only once a year to atone for his and the people's sins. According to an ancient rabbinic tradition, the high priest would enter with such great trepidation that other priests would tie a gold cord around his leg. That way, they could drag him out if he dropped dead. Imagine the fear the high priest experienced as he washed his body, changed into the proper garments, and slowly pulled back the curtain to the sacred inner chamber. We have no such cause to fear. God invites all of us to enter the new "most holy place," the heavenly sanctuary, where we have unlimited access to him.

1. Whose blood gives us access to the most holy place (v. 19)?

2. Scan Matthew 27:50–51. What is the new curtain (Hebrews 10:20)? Why did God destroy the old curtain? What does that tell you about God and his affection for his people?

DIGGING DEEPER

Read Leviticus 8 to see how the priests consecrated themselves to enter into the Lord's presence and make sacrifices on behalf of themselves and the people. What strikes you? How does this change the way you think about what Jesus did so that we can have an all-access pass into the most holy place?

3. In Hebrews 10:22, the author exhorts us to "draw near to God" in two ways. What are they? Why does God want us to have these heart attitudes in place before we draw near to Him?

Sin stains. Like a glob of mustard down the front of your shirt, sin leaves a mark that no laundry detergent can remove. But verse 22 reveals that Jesus's precious blood accomplishes a remarkable feat—it cleanses us from a guilty conscience and washes our bodies with pure water.

4. When was the last time you suffered from a guilty conscience? How did you feel? Do you tend to hold on to past sins as if Jesus's blood is insufficient to cleanse you? If so, why?

I began listing the sins he'd forgiven. One by one I thanked God for forgiving my stumbles and tumbles. My motives were pure and my heart was thankful, but my understanding of God was wrong. It was when I used the word remember that it hit me . . . "Remember the time I . . ." I was about to thank God for another act of mercy. But I stopped. Something was wrong. The word *remember* seemed displaced. It was an off-key note in a sonata, a misplaced word in a poem. . . . I remembered his words. "For I will forgive their wickedness and will remember their sins no more" (Hebrews 8:12).[3]
—Max Lucado

KEEP ON LOVING ONE ANOTHER DEEPLY

5. Next, the author encourages us to "spur one another on toward love and good deeds" (v. 24). Make a list of specific ways you can do this.

OPTIONAL

If you are needlessly continuing to carry guilt, write a short prayer thanking God for making a way for you to enter blamelessly into his presence and for the privilege of moving forward cleansed.

6. Who has inspired you to do more good works or be more loving? What about them encourages you to better live out your faith?

We can never realize the likeness of Christ by ourselves alone; we will never transform the world as individuals; we will never discover fullness of life in Christ if we stay solo. We are distinct as people of God because we were made to live in dependence on the head and interdependently with the diverse parts of the body.[4]
—Julie Gorman

The vast majority of the Roman Empire worshipped the emperor first and the ancient gods and goddesses second. Christians represented a small minority of the population and wanted nothing to do with these false gods.

7. What does the author advise the Christians to do to strengthen their endurance as a minority group (v. 25)? How would this practice help? Why did they especially need encouragement at this time?

8. These first-century believers lived in a place where persecution was on the rise. Have you found yourself in situations where it's harder to be a Christian now than in the past? What examples come to mind? How might seriously applying the instruction in verse 25 help you represent Christ well in those situations?

Community is great. And then the people show up. When people show up, a group becomes the place where mess happens. But that mess may prove to be the answer to our prayers. It may become the catalyst for, the byproduct of and the environment in which discipleship happens. . . . We become the body of Christ broken and battered and bloodied and poured out for those around us.[5]
—Heather Zempel

9. What has been your experience with Christian small groups in the past? Life-giving? Well-led, organized, and helpful? Disappointing? Poorly led, disorganized, or a waste of time? Can you discern why?

BIG RED WARNING FLAG FOUR

APOSTASY RESULTS IN HORRENDOUS CONSEQUENCES!

 Read Hebrews 10:26–31.

Hebrews 10:26–31 presents the most severe and frightening of all the warnings. The author cautions his audience that suffering and loss await all who backslide because God pursues his disobedient children like the hound of heaven. They also stand to lose eternal rewards at the bema judgment. First-century Jewish Christians had a choice to make. Would they suffer discipline from God or persecution from the Romans? The author challenges them to stand firm in their faith by illustrating that the consequences of backsliding will be worse than any hardship they might endure at the hands of the Roman government.

10. What does the pronoun *we* in verse 26 tell us about the author's intended audience? Also note the pronoun in the last quote of verse 30. Why is this important?

11. What awaits believers who abandon following Jesus and fall back into a life of deliberate and continual sin (vv. 26–27)?

The judgment in view here will take place at the judgment seat of Christ, not the great white throne. It is the judgment of Christians (2 Corinthians 5:10), not of unbelievers (Revelation 20:11–15). It will result in loss of reward, not loss of salvation. The author uses the same word, *fire*, to symbolize divine judgment. God will test believers' works with fire at the judgment seat of Christ but will punish unbelievers at the great white throne judgment.[7]

> The writer was urging mutual accountability, since . . . "The Day" that is "drawing near" is the day that we will give an account of ourselves to God (cf. v. 37). This may have been, partially, an allusion to the destruction of Jerusalem in A.D. 70 for the original readers. But it is probably primarily an allusion to the judgment seat of Christ.[6]
> —Thomas Constable

> An apostate is a believer who falls away from their faith in words or actions such that they are basically indistinguishable from a nonbeliever. Another word often used to describe them is "backslider." They break intimate fellowship with God, hide their testimony, and often forsake their faith community.

12. According to Hebrews 10:28, what happened to those who rejected the law of Moses in the Old Testament and sinned defiantly (Deuteronomy 17:2–7)?

The author explains that willful rebels under the old covenant lost their physical lives, but willful rebels under the new covenant face an even greater consequence, a long-term consequence: the loss of eternal rewards at the judgment seat of Christ (2 Corinthians 5:10).

13. What three deliberate sins does the author describe in Hebrews 10:29 that reap loss of eternal rewards? Fill in the blanks below and give an example of each.

who has _____ the _____ underfoot

who has _____ the blood of the

_____ that _____ them

who has _____ the Spirit of _____

14. Reread verses 30 and 31. How do these verses make you feel? What do you think the author is attempting to teach the audience? Do these words motivate you or discourage you? Why?

 **Read 1 Corinthians 11:27–32.**

15. In his letter admonishing the Corinthians, Paul chastises the believers for their attitude when taking communion.

   What does he call their actions and attitude in verse 27?

   What has happened to some of them as a result (v. 30)?

   Why does God discipline his children this way (vv. 31–32)?

Swindoll describes the apostate this way: "This isn't just a stumble, a season of rebellion, or a constant struggle against temptation and sin. We all experience these. This is outright opposition against the gracious, loving, merciful Father."[9]

16. Once someone has a true conversion experience, how secure is their salvation (Romans 8:33–39)? Do you feel secure in the Lord? Why or why not?

 **Read Hebrews 10:32–39.**

After these sober admonitions, the author encourages his readers by reminding them of their past successes in staying faithful amidst extreme suffering and persecution.

> God disciplines His children severely when they cross the line and reach that point of no return—when they continue in willful defiance of Him. He may justly deprive them of their physical lives (Acts 5:1–10; 1 Cor. 11:27–30; 1 Jn 5:16); in any case, they will lose heavenly reward before the judgment seat of Christ (1 Cor. 3:15; 2 Cor. 5:10).[8]
> —Charles Swindoll

DIGGING DEEPER

In 2 Peter 2:17–22, Peter describes believers who became apostates and abandoned Christ. What were they like? What happened to them? How does Peter feel about what awaits them at the judgment seat of Christ?

> It's doubtful that you will ever be tempted to exchange your faith for an ancient system of priests and sacrifices. But you will be tempted to exchange it for something inferior. If you are reading Hebrews, be reminded: Once you've known the best, why settle for anything less?[10]
> —Max Lucado

DIGGING DEEPER

Let's discover together how God treats his stubborn sheep when they return to the fold. Read Luke 15. What do the three parables tell you about your heavenly Father? What is his posture toward sinners (v. 20)? How does he respond when his lost children come home (vv. 22–24)?

Affliction is a treasure, and scarce any man hath enough of it. No man hath affliction enough that is not matured and ripened by and made fit for God by that affliction.[11]

—John Donne

DIGGING DEEPER

Read the following passages: 1 Corinthians 9:24–25; 1 Thessalonians 2:19; 2 Timothy 4:8; 1 Peter 5:4; Revelation 2:10. What do these verses have in common? How do they relate to Hebrews 10:35?

17. Specifically, what had they endured with admirable stamina, shining as a bright witness for Christ in a dark culture (vv. 32–34)? Do these realities help you understand why some were tempted to abandon their faith?

18. Have you ever experienced any of these kinds of persecution? How do you think you would respond if you did? How can you prepare for these possibilities in the future?

19. What future events does the author discuss to encourage us to persevere during struggles and temptations (vv. 35–39)? What quality do we need to stand strong in tough times (v. 36)? What is the Lord teaching you through these daunting passages in Hebrews?

BE ENCOURAGED BY THEIR LEGACY OF FAITH

Throughout Hebrews the author pressed the recipients to persevere through extreme persecution as Christians made the name of Christ known in a hostile first-century Roman culture. Ultimately, these courageous men and women brought down a worldwide empire built on sheer might, fear, and cruelty through their strong faith, humility, and service. To strengthen his readers and future believers, now the author provides a long list of God's people whose valor and devotion encourage all of us. This section has traditionally been called the "Hall of Faith."

Some people believe that Christianity finds its roots in myths and fairy tales. Some skeptics have accused believers of parking their brains at the door before they enter the sanctuary. The author of Hebrews wants us to see that nothing could be further from the truth. Faith is not an act of forcing oneself to believe something for which no evidence exists. That's not faith—that's ignorance. Rather, faith is the logical step one takes after beholding the vast wealth of evidence all around us. Let's consider the evidence together.

 **Read Hebrews 11.**

20. How does the author define *faith* (v. 1)? How would you define it?

> Though the "things" are only "hoped for" and "not seen" at present, the eye of faith can see them, and the hand of faith can grasp them. Faith is more mighty than any of our senses, or than all our senses combined.[12]
> —Charles Spurgeon

21. Choose three heroes of the faith from Hebrews 11 and describe why you believe the author included them in his Hall of Faith. Why are their examples especially meaningful to you? How will remembering their lives encourage us all to persevere? (If you need more information, consult a Bible concordance and find more details about their story.)

22. What motivated our forefathers and foremothers of the faith (vv. 26, 35, 39–40)? What will we all inherit together (Revelation 20:4–6; 21:1–4; 22:3–5, 12)?

❋ Read Hebrews 12:1–3.

23. Who are the people who surround us, cheering us on as we live out our faith in a hostile, dark world (v. 1)?

24. Picture the scene the author paints in verses 1–3. What can we do so we will not grow weary or lose heart? Who is the supreme example of perfect faith, and what did he do to inspire us to persevere?

25. The author says we should "throw off everything that hinders and the sin that so easily entangles" (v. 1). Notice these include hindrances that might not necessarily be sin. For example, nothing is inherently wrong with scrolling through social media. But if, when you look through the pictures of others' lives, you find yourself comparing and despairing, the author calls you to throw it off. What else hinders your progress in your walk with Christ?

26. Mentally scroll through the memories of your past. Can you think of circumstances or situations where God has carried you? In the space below, write your own "by faith" statement. Insert your name and describe how God has worked with you, for you, and through you.

By faith,

_____

_____

YOUR FUTURE INHERITANCE

The price of gold hovers around two thousand dollars an ounce, and gold bricks weigh about thirty pounds. This means that one gold brick costs almost a million dollars. Great, you say, but what's the point? You have no plans to buy a gold brick, and neither do we. But gold is in your future—if you are a faithful follower of Christ.

Hebrews 11:10 tells us that Abraham lived as a tent-dwelling foreigner in Canaan because he was "looking forward to the city with foundations, whose architect and builder is God." In Revelation 21:16–20, John describes that city in glorious detail. See verses 16–18:

> The city was laid out like a square, as long as it was wide. . . . The angel measured the wall using human measurement, and it was 144 cubits thick. The wall was made of jasper, and the city of pure gold, as pure as glass.

The entire city—1,380 square miles—from the roads, to the foundations, to the buildings—is made of the purest gold. And one brick of gold costs nearly a million dollars.

The patriarchs, the prophets of old, the apostles, and countless believers through the centuries have sacrificed in the here and now because their spirit has glimpsed the there and then. Jesus said, "Do not store up for yourselves treasures on earth, where moths and vermin destroy, and where thieves break in and steal. But store up for yourselves treasures in heaven, where moths and vermin do not destroy, and where thieves do not break in and steal" (Matthew 6:19–20). He also said, "And everyone who has left houses or brothers or sisters or father or mother or wife or children or fields for my sake will receive a hundred times as much and will inherit eternal life" (19:29).

Paul tells us to build our lives on the foundation of Jesus Christ and to use gold, silver, and costly stones that represent the good works God created us to do, which will result in priceless rewards in the age to come. Revelation 20:6 reveals that faithful believers will "reign with him for a thousand years" in a renewed kingdom on the earth ruled by King Jesus.

As we saw, the Bible also pictures the heavenly city made of gold. Should we understand the imagery literally or metaphorically? We don't know for sure. But we can know this: when we cross the threshold of eternity and enter into the presence of the Lord, what we find will be so splendid, so glorious, so breathtaking that the most precious materials in this world will be as common as drywall. Let this reality give you the grit to live out your faith until the judgment seat of Christ, when you stand before Jesus to receive your inheritance.

Better Because He Never Disappoints Like Earthly Parents

REJOICE IN YOUR PERFECT HEAVENLY FATHER

by Leah Holder Green

OPTIONAL:

Memorize Hebrews 12:11

No discipline seems pleasant at the time, but painful. Later on, however, it produces a harvest of righteousness and peace for those who have been trained by it.

When I was a college freshman, a classmate invited me to join his study group, but when I knocked on his dorm room door, I was shocked to discover the "study group" included only him and me. When he invited me inside, my heart began to race. Although my father was over 150 miles away, I immediately thought of him. He would not approve of me going into this young man's room alone. So I didn't. The young man continued to pursue me, though, until I became afraid and called my father. He called the campus police but learned they would not intervene. I thought that meant I had no protection.

Yet one day, as I was exiting the class we shared, I saw my dad standing in the hall! I pointed out my male classmate. My father didn't touch him or say a word. He just looked at him. The culprit saw my six-foot-six dad's glare and walked in the opposite direction. Guess what happened? That young man never bothered me again. This incident illustrates my relationship with my dad—I'm blessed with a good earthly father.

What comes to mind when you think of your father? Some have warm thoughts of love and gratitude. These women likely grew up with supportive fathers who lived up to their duty to care for, protect, and guide them. For others, thinking of their fathers stirs up bitter and painful thoughts. These women grew up with absent, abusive, or otherwise disappointing fathers. For still others, thinking of their fathers engenders sadness, not because of anything their fathers did but because their fathers have passed away. No matter what kinds of fathers we've had—good, bad, absent, or otherwise—none of them were perfect.

But through Jesus we gain a perfect Father in heaven. He thinks perfectly, speaks perfectly, loves us perfectly, and treats us perfectly all the time. This relationship comes with big-time implications, blessings, and responsibilities. In this lesson, we'll explore these ramifications while we learn that everything, including our relationship with our heavenly Father, is better through Jesus.

BETTER CORRECTION

1. Some of us experienced shortsighted, senseless discipline from our earthly parents. How were you disciplined growing up? Healthily? Fairly? Unhealthily? Harshly? If you can, discern why.

2. How does your relationship with your earthly father impact your relationship with your heavenly Father? Are you more likely to view God as a loving father with your best interest at heart or as a doting Santa Claus, distant judge, ruthless police officer, or cold taskmaster?

3. How do you typically respond when you believe God is disciplining you? How do you think your view of God affects you when journeying through seasons of trial and hardship?

❋ Read Hebrews 12:4–13.

The author begins this section by rebuking his readers.

4. In their suffering and struggles, what have they forgotten (vv. 4–6)?

5. What do you think it means that they "have not yet resisted to the point of shedding [their] blood" (v. 4)? Who might the author be talking about (9:12–14)?

6. In verses 5 and 6, the author quotes Proverbs 3:11–12. Although this proverb concerns discipline, why do you think the author refers to it as a "word of encouragement that addresses you as a father addresses his son" (Hebrews 12:5)?

7. Are you tempted to lose heart when you experience the Lord's discipline (v. 5)? If so, why and in what ways?

8. What makes it easy or difficult for you to believe that "the Lord disciplines the one he loves" (v. 6)?

9. If someone never experiences God's discipline, what does that indicate about their relationship with him (vv. 7–8)?

It may come as a shock to many Christians to discover that there lies ahead of them a life in which God, precisely because he is treating us as sons and daughters, will refuse to spoil us or ignore us, will refuse to let us get away for ever with rebellion or folly, with sin or stupidity. He has his ways of alerting his children to the fact that they should either pause and think again, or turn round and go in the opposite direction, or get down on their knees and repent.[4]
—N. T. Wright

10. What is the end goal of discipline (vv. 9–11)?

Eat the fruit of sorrow, even if it is bitter. This fruit, that you can only eat now, has nutrients in it that you can't get any other way. . . .

There are nutrients that we draw out of seasons of suffering that are strengthening to the bones of our faith and sweetening to the marrow of our faith. . . . Go ahead and eat them. As long as God keeps you in that season, don't waste it by wishing and wishing, wishing you'd be out of it. Go ahead and eat the fruit that grows on that tree alone.[5]
—John Piper

11. How have you seen God produce a harvest of righteousness or peace through past seasons of painful discipline? Describe what happened.

Swindoll writes, "God's loving hand of fatherly discipline produces *assurance* by demonstrating that we are his children (12:7–8). It results in *maturity* by deepening and enhancing our spiritual lives (12:9). It leads to *conformity* with God's character by continuing to draw us closer to Him throughout our lives (12:10). And it results in *holiness* by pruning us in order to produce spiritual fruit (12:11)."[6]

12. In light of the four benefits listed above, how should we respond to discipline (vv. 12–13)?

BETTER LIVING IN THE LONG RUN

Read Hebrews 12:14–17.

Discipline, trials, and struggles in the Christian life ultimately lead to a better race—strong character and holy living. Now the author provides additional advice to help us reach the finish line successfully.

13. Why do you think the author encourages us to "make every effort to live in peace with everyone and to be holy" (v. 14)? Why is this especially important when we are living through personal struggles and in difficult times?

14. How can bitterness cause trouble and defile people (v. 15)?

What in the world does the author mean in verses 12 and 13 by "strengthen your feeble arms and weak knees" so that you may not be lame but healed? The author is referring back to his imagery of running a race in 12:1–3. If you are out of shape but decide to run a marathon, you know the preparation process will involve ice packs and heating pads. Your joints will ache. Your muscles will be sore. But if you train wisely, you'll build up your strength, your joints and muscles will heal, and when the time comes you'll be ready for the race. Enduring tough times requires the same kind of discipline. It's painful, but it prepares you for a harvest of righteous success ahead.

15. Have you ever let a "bitter root" grow up and cause trouble in your life? If so, describe the circumstances and results. (No names, please.) What would you do differently next time?

Next, the author briefly mentions sexual immorality in verse 16 in connection with an Old Testament account of twin brothers, Jacob and Esau, in Genesis 25:19–34. Esau was born first, so he was entitled to a greater birthright than Jacob, who was born a few seconds later. Jacob, however, was determined to get Esau's birthright (and later his blessing). Jacob cooked Esau's favorite stew and then talked his twin into trading his birthright for that bowl of stew (Hebrews 12:16–17).

16. What does Esau's impulsive decision teach us in relation to the author's admonition to beware of sexual immorality?

DIGGING DEEPER

Read the account of Jacob and Esau from Genesis 25:19–34 for context. What else do you learn from this story to help you "live in peace with everyone and to be holy" (Hebrews 12:14)?

In *The Message*, Eugene Peterson paraphrases Hebrews 12:16 this way: "Watch out for the Esau syndrome: trading away God's lifelong gift in order to satisfy a short-term appetite."

17. What did Esau exchange for his inheritance rights? What lesser things do some people today exchange for their spiritual inheritance and future rewards from God?

18. Are there areas of unholiness in your life that you need to confess? When are you tempted to gratify immediate desires instead of persevering in righteous living?

A BETTER MOUNTAIN EXPERIENCE

 Read Hebrews 12:18–25.

Like many sections we have already studied, the author again assumes his audience's extensive knowledge of the Old Testament. Without retelling the full story, he references an event from Exodus 19.

Three months after God led the Israelites out of Egypt, he brought them to Mount Sinai, where they received the Ten Commandments. The Israelites were to consecrate themselves for three days in anticipation of encountering God. They blocked off the mountain and stood at a distance in order to be protected from God's holiness. God descended on the mountain with thunder, lightning, thick clouds, a trumpet blast, and an earthquake. All the people, including Moses, were utterly terrified, but they ultimately received God's commandments and were set apart as his holy nation.

The author of Hebrews compares and contrasts the Israelites' time at Mount Sinai with how we can approach God at Mount Zion today and in the future. Because of Jesus, our experience is both similar and different from the Israelites'. Most significantly, the blood of Jesus makes a way for us to sense God's presence now and for eternity in a brand-new way.

19. Reread the Israelites' encounter with God on Mount Sinai (Hebrews 12:18–21), and immerse yourself in the scene, imagining each detail. How would you respond if you encountered that scene today?

DIGGING DEEPER

Read Exodus 19–20 to learn more about the event on Mount Sinai. Do you approach the Lord with fear or joy? Why?

20. Verses 22–24 picture a future time when all believers will gather on God's holy mountain. Where is it? How does Mount Zion compare to Mount Sinai?

21. The author lists what we'll find when we gather at Mount Zion (vv. 22–24). What will we see there?

A BETTER MOUNTAINTOP EXPERIENCE

Read Isaiah 2:1–5.

22. The earth's landscape will change when King Jesus inaugurates his millennial kingdom on the earth.

What is one aspect of that change (vv. 1–2)?

Who will teach us the King's ways, and how can we live together in beauty, harmony, and righteousness (v. 3)?

Describe how King Jesus's leadership will change people's lives and the interactions between nations (v. 4).

If King Jesus ruled the world today, how do you think news reporting and media would look different?

BIG RED WARNING FLAG FIVE

Wake up and listen to him!

 Read Hebrews 12:25–29.

This section contains the fifth and final warning. Jesus is loving, but he's no pushover. The author implores his audience not to "refuse him who speaks" (v. 25). In other words, listen seriously and intently to God. Don't disregard what God has said through his Son and his Word, because doing so results in horrendous personal consequences, including loss of rewards in the future kingdom. These exciting rewards will determine what believers will do in the kingdom.

This final warning still relates to the previous section about Mount Sinai and Mount Zion. On Mount Sinai, God spoke through Moses. However, the exodus generation did not listen and were refused entry into the promised land. But now God "has spoken to us by his Son" (1:2). Today, God invites us to enter his promised rest (3:7–11) in the millennial kingdom and the new heaven and the new earth—a rest that lasts for eternity. But only if we listen with an intent to act!

23. What circumstances might tempt you to disregard the Lord's words? Do you struggle to quiet your own thoughts and instead listen to what God might be speaking to you through his Word, Spirit, and wise people? How could you grow in this area?

Is it not wonderful that it should be written, "We are receiving a kingdom"? What a gift to receive! This is a divine gift; we have received, not a pauper's pension, but a kingdom that cannot be moved. . . . We are not under the yoke of Moses, but we are the subjects of King Jesus, whose yoke is easy and whose burden is light. The kingdom of Jesus will never end while time shall last, for He is the King Eternal, and immortal; neither will His laws be changed, nor shall His subjects die.[8]
—Charles Spurgeon

This is what the Lord Almighty says: "In a little while I will once more shake the heavens and the earth, the sea and the dry land. I will shake all nations, and what is desired by all nations will come, and I will fill this house with glory. . . . The glory of this present house will be greater than the glory of the former house. . . . And in this place I will grant peace."
—The prophet Haggai (2:6–9)

24. What will faithful believers inherit in the millennial kingdom? How should we live now as a result? (12:28; Revelation 20:6)

25. Why do you think the author ends with the phrase "our 'God is a consuming fire'" (Hebrews 12:29; Deuteronomy 4:24)?

THE PRODUCT OF PAIN

by Hannah Beckwith Beasley

I gave my life to Jesus when I was fourteen years old. Later that year I dealt with complicated and unexplainable health concerns. As a Christian, shouldn't my life be getting easier? I reacted with depression and hopelessness over physicians who initially didn't take me seriously, endless doctors' appointments and tests, surgeries, physical therapy, and lengthy periods of recuperation. What began as joint pain and fatigue has turned into a life-altering chronic disease. Now, ten years later, I'm the wife of a minister, mom, and seminary student, and I still live with daily, persistent, and continual pain.

In the thirteen years after my initial diagnosis, in an attempt to understand how God would allow this overwhelming illness to disrupt my life, I devoured Scripture, attended Bible studies, read books on suffering, and listened to Bible scholars teach on the subject. I had committed to follow Jesus, and I wanted to figure out how to do that well, even in the midst of this ongoing distress.

Before my conversion, I lived for my own happiness, avoiding discomfort and pursuing personal desires above all else. However, through this ordeal I realized that God cares more about my holiness than my happiness. He desires for me to learn from him and follow Jesus not just when it's easy but in every moment and in all seasons.

After many years of walking this difficult road, I still struggle to understand God's plans and purposes in my suffering. And yet, he has sustained my faith, teaching me about his character and showing me that he is worthy of my trust and adoration. Some days are easier than others, both physically and spiritually. But he has faithfully "trained" me through my struggles to look to him alone, put my hope in him alone, and follow him alone. While I still have much to learn, and many areas of my heart still need refinement, I see that he's been cultivating a supernatural strength and peace as a by-product of my pain, and I trust he'll find ways to use it to glorify himself in the future.

Walk the Better Way

First-century Christians who read this letter were a lot like us. They lived during a time when many people in the outside world looked down on them and misunderstood their beliefs. Shaking in their sandals, they were tempted to abandon their faith rather than risk the culture's scorn that was edging closer and closer to persecution. Like many Christian leaders today, the author of Hebrews observed these trends and wrote a magnificent appeal, answering the question that Peter asked and answered when many were deserting Jesus: "Lord, to whom shall we go? You [and you alone] have the words of eternal life" (John 6:68).

We've made our way through a challenging book together, and our great desire and prayer is that this study will strengthen your resolve to remain forever faithful to your King. In addition, we hope that you will always remember the great theme of Hebrews—that compared to whoever or whatever else you are tempted to worship and follow, Christ is better because he is superior in every way.

> Christ is superior to Moses and all other human heroes.
> Christ is superior to angels and all other spiritualities.
> Christ offers superior rest.
> Christ is superior to Melchizedek.
> Christ is superior to the Old Testament high priests.
> Christ offers a superior once-for-all sacrifice.
> Christ fulfilled and is superior to the law.
> Christ initiated a superior new covenant.
> Christ is superior because he never disappoints like human leaders.
> Christ is superior because he never disappoints like human parents.
> Christ is superior because he alone grants us 24/7 access into the heavenly sanctuary.
> Christ, in his person and work, is superior to everyone and everything.

OPTIONAL

Memorize Hebrews 13:20–21

Now may the God of peace, who through the blood of the eternal covenant brought back from the dead our Lord Jesus, that great Shepherd of the sheep, equip you with everything good for doing his will, and may he work in us what is pleasing to him, through Jesus Christ, to whom be glory for ever and ever. Amen.

All of us—whether Jew or Gentile—can sense the heat rising in our increasingly anti-Christian culture and feel the pressure to conform to the values and priorities of this darkening world. . . . We need to come to grips with the sufficiency of Christ and His absolute superiority over all things. We need to stand and say a pledge of allegiance to the Lord who bought us with His own blood.[1]
—Charles Swindoll

Now the Hebrews author tops off these great theological themes with a practical question: In light of these magnificent truths, how should we then live?

 **Read Hebrews 13:1–3.**

LIVE OUT LOVE INSIDE THE CHURCH

1. What does the author want us to continue doing in the community of faith, especially in challenging times (v. 1)? Why is this important (Philippians 2:1–4; Hebrews 10:24–25; John 13:34–35)?

LIVE OUT LOVE OUTSIDE THE CHURCH

In the ancient world, inns and hostels were seedbeds of immorality and danger. Smart travelers were left with few options, except to rely on the hospitality of kind people to take them in and offer a warm bed and a hot meal. This custom gave outsiders the opportunity to experience how Christians lived and worshipped. Thus, hospitality became an important form of evangelism.

2. Since hospitality was an important virtue in ancient Near Eastern culture, the Hebrews author encouraged believers to act hospitably (Hebrews 13:2). What comes to mind when you think of hospitality? Is hospitality limited to serving guests in your home? How does Jesus describe hospitality in Matthew 25:35–40?

3. Who else should we remember when we are hospitable (Hebrews 13:3)? Why are these intentional attitudes and actions critical to our Christian witness in the culture?

4. Are you a hospitable person? If so, what are the benefits? If not, what hinders you?

Christianity was, and still should be, the religion of the open door.[2]
—William Barclay

DIGGING DEEPER

The author says, "Some people have shown hospitality to angels without knowing it" (v. 2). Read the following verses—Genesis 18:1–8; 19:1–3; Luke 1:8–13—and describe the angelic encounters. What are angels like? Did the people in the story know they were in the presence of divine beings? If so, how do you think they knew?

Some people will never entertain angels unaware, for they never entertain anybody. May we be given to hospitality, for that should be part of the character of saints.[3]
—Charles Spurgeon

RESIST THE TEMPTATIONS OF SEX AND MONEY

 Read Hebrews 13:4–6.

5. Contrast the value of marriage inside and outside the church today. Why do you think so many in our culture have adopted such a low view of marriage? How have you been personally affected by this reality? Why do you think God cares deeply about fidelity in marriage?

Marriage is to be respected and honoured by all, and nobody must try to break into the sexual union of husband and wife. The pagan world of the first century was every bit as sexually promiscuous as the Western world of the twenty-first century, and Christians are called today, as they were then, to stand out, to be deeply counter-cultural. . . . It is all too frequent that those who degrade themselves and other people by indulging in sex outside its proper context carry bitter regrets and long-lasting emotional scars.[4]
—N. T. Wright

6. Money and materialism were just as much a snare in the first century as they are now. The word *content* means to have enough or to be satisfied. In a world that tells us *more* is the key to happiness, contentment can be elusive. What does verse 5 advise?

7. Are you content? Why or why not? What does Proverbs 30:7–9 recommend?

8. Why does the author of Hebrews tell his hearers that they can be content (13:5–6)? What does Paul counsel us (1 Corinthians 7:17–24)? How does Paul overcome his struggles to be content (Philippians 4:11–13)? How might these verses help you if you struggle to be satisfied with your life as it is?

HONOR YOUR LEADERS

✳ Read Hebrews 13:7, 17–19.

9. How are believers instructed to treat their leaders in verses 7 and 17? Why? How can you bless the leaders who serve you (v. 18)?

The word "imitate" is translated from the Greek *mimeomai*, where we get "mimic," "mime," and "mimeograph" (for those of us old enough to remember the days before copy machines!).

10. What leaders have influenced your faith? What about them do you admire? What qualities do they display that you would like to imitate?

DIGGING DEEPER

Read 1 Timothy 3:1–7; Titus 1:5–9; and 1 Peter 5:1–3. List ten characteristics of godly leaders. While not all of these apply to everyone, they reveal God's expectations for leaders who help us discern the false teachers in our midst or on our devices.

11. This past decade we've witnessed many fallen leaders, including Christians. Even those we trust the most are capable of grievous sin. Ultimately, only Christ is the perfect leader. What does verse 8 reveal about his nature, and how might that comfort us today?

Read Hebrews 13:9–17.

Throughout Hebrews, the author has warned his first-century audience not to be taken in by Judaizers—people who were attempting to woo them back to their former empty religion focused on externals (the Mosaic law, animal offerings, dietary restrictions, and temple worship). Today, our temptation is different but equally destructive—under the pressure of acceptance and tolerance, we may abandon our grace-based faith and buy into the culture's promises of satisfaction and fulfillment.

12. Now the author of Hebrews reminds believers to be wary of "strange teachings" related to certain unclean foods. Instead of focusing on externals, what does the author prescribe in verse 9? Why is the author's suggestion so much better?

Those who cling to the external and ceremonial observances of religion have no right to the privileges that belong to those who come to the spiritual altar; they cannot share that secret. Those whose religion consists in outward rites and ceremonies can never eat of the spiritual altar at which spiritual men eat, for they do not understand the Scripture and they still serve the Mosaic tabernacle.[5]
—Charles Spurgeon

WE WORSHIP AT A DIFFERENT ALTAR "OUTSIDE THE CAMP"

In verses 9–16, the words *altar*, *tabernacle*, and *animal blood* would have immediately reminded first-century Jews and Jewish Christians about the Levitical sacrificial system, where once a year, in the Jerusalem temple, the high priest offered animal sacrifices on the Day of Atonement.

13. When Hebrews was written, the Jewish high priest was still offering animal sacrifices on the temple altar in Jerusalem. Today we Christians worship at a superior altar (v. 10). Where is our altar (9:11–12, 24)? Why is our altar superior? Why aren't the Judaizers allowed to worship there?

We can anticipate receiving God's grace through Jesus because "we have an altar" to nourish us that is forbidden to the Levitical priests who serve "the tent," the earthly sanctuary (cf. 8:4–5). . . . Our "altar" symbolizes Jesus' sacrifice on the cross "outside the gate" of Jerusalem (13:12). To "eat" from this altar is to benefit from his sacrifice offered once for all "to sanctify the people."[6]
—Dennis Johnson

14. Where were the animal bodies disposed of after they were sacrificed (13:11; Leviticus 16:27–28)? Specifically, where was Jesus crucified (Matthew 27:31–33; John 19:20)? Why is this significant?

15. Jesus suffered outside the place where people lived and gathered. According to verse 13, why must believers "go to him outside the camp"? What can faithful Christians expect when they pledge allegiance to Jesus?

16. What are the benefits of standing strong against opposition when you follow Christ?

James 1:2–4

Matthew 5:10–11

DIGGING DEEPER

List the promises Scripture provides to help believers through times of trials and opposition. See John 16:33; James 1:12; and Hebrews 13:5 to get started.

Matthew 16:24

1 Peter 1:6–8

17. Can you recall a time when you learned a valuable lesson by standing strong against opposition? If so, please share it with the group.

WE POSSESS A GLORIOUS AND SECURE FUTURE

Never has it been more important for God's people to understand the prophetic word and to look for Christ's appearing. People everywhere today have sobering, searching questions about what the future holds. God's Word is the only place we can find sure answers. Yet, at the very time when serious study . . . is most needed, its importance has diminished in many churches and in the lives of many Christians.[7]
—Mark Hitchcock

18. Have you ever felt that you just don't belong in this world? There's a reason. According to Hebrews 13:14, we are strangers and temporary residents here. But we can anticipate a wonderful future that Jesus is preparing for each of us now. What do you know about this "city that is to come" (v. 14; Revelation 21:1–4, 9–24)?

To inform and inspire Bible students about their glorious futures, consider studying the Discover Together Bible Study *1 and 2 Thessalonians: Discovering Hope in a Promised Future* by Sue Edwards.

HOW SHOULD WE THEN LIVE?

19. Because of what Christ did for us on the cross, we are no longer bound to the Levitical sacrificial system. Instead, what kinds of sacrifices do we offer every day out of overwhelming gratitude for what Jesus did for us (Hebrews 13:15–16; Romans 12:1–2)? How do we do this?

DIGGING DEEPER

Read Psalm 43. What is the author's mindset in verses 1 and 2? What does he do in verse 3? What is the author's advice to himself in verse 5? How does this psalm relate to Hebrews 13:15?

At this, Job got up and tore his robe and shaved his head. Then he fell to the ground in worship and said: "Naked I came from my mother's womb, and naked I will depart. The Lord gave and the Lord has taken away; may the name of the Lord be praised."
　　　　　　　—Job 1:20–21

FINAL THOUGHTS

 Read Hebrews 13:20–25.

20. The benediction in verses 20–21 reads like a prayer. Fill in the blanks to discover what the author asks God on your behalf:

Now may the God of _____, who through the

_____ of the _____

brought back from the dead our Lord Jesus, that great

_____ of the sheep, _____

you with everything good for doing _____,

and may he _____ in us what is pleasing to him,

through Jesus Christ, to whom be glory for ever and ever. Amen.

Will the Lord be pleased with thousands of rams, with ten thousand rivers of olive oil? Shall I offer my firstborn for my transgression, the fruit of my body for the sin of my soul? He has shown you, O mortal, what is good. And what does the Lord require of you? To act justly and to love mercy and to walk humbly with your God.
　　　　　　　—The prophet Micah (6:7–8)

What assurance does Philippians 2:13 give us as we attempt to live out this benediction?

Throughout our study, the author has built the case that Jesus is better than everything else that you may be tempted to believe in and follow. Review the list of "superiors" in the introduction to this lesson.

21. Do you tend to consider anything else better than Jesus? If so, what and why?

22. Write a prayer asking Jesus to deepen your love for him and to continue to show himself as better, especially in the areas of your life listed above.

23. Share with the group the most valuable insights you will retain from the book of Hebrews. What did you learn that will stay with you long-term—a month from now? A year from now? Ten years from now?

The author of Hebrews began with a tribute to God's ultimate word spoken in and through Jesus Christ. He ends with a tribute to God's ultimate work in raising the "Lord Jesus from the dead" (13:20 NKJV) and for equipping us "with everything good for doing his will" (verse 21). Throughout the letter, the author has asked us to look back to the Old Testament—not with the intention of reliving *those* days, but to help us live in *these* days. God filled the history of his people with lessons that illuminate his magnificent plan for all people. Through the words of Hebrews we hear the voices of the ages, urging us to keep the faith in our times.[9]

—Max Lucado

OUR HOPE IN THE SUBSTANCE, NOT IN THE SHADOW

As a young girl with undiagnosed anxiety, I (Rebecca) discovered great solace in books. A voracious reader, I could devour a novel in an afternoon, and to my busy mother's exasperation, I often did. My library card was among my most treasured possessions. To this day, winding through rows of weathered books, breathing in the musty smell of aged pages, remains a favorite pastime.

Reading opens a portal to another world where the laws of nature and science need not apply. I tumbled down a rabbit hole with Alice, discovered a secret garden with Mary Lennox, and buried my face in Aslan's great mane with Lucy and Susan.

C. S. Lewis's seven-novel saga details the creation of the fictional country Narnia in *The Magician's Nephew* to its eventual demise in *The Last Battle*. Students well-versed in Scripture will see biblical themes weaved throughout. Surely the author drew from Hebrews 8:1–6 when he penned the following words in the final book:

> "Kings and Queens," he cried, "we have all been blind. We are only beginning to see where we are. From up there I have seen it all—Ettinsmuir, Beaversdam, the Great River, and Cair Paravel still shining on the edge of the Eastern Sea. Narnia is not dead. This is Narnia."

> "But how can it be?" said Peter. "For Aslan told us older ones that we should never return to Narnia, and here we are."

> "Yes," said Eustace. "And we saw it all destroyed and the sun put out."

> "And it's all so different," said Lucy.

> "The Eagle is right," said the Lord Digory. "Listen, Peter. When Aslan said you could never go back to Narnia, he meant the Narnia you were thinking of. But that was not the real Narnia. That had a beginning and an end. It was only a shadow or a copy of the real Narnia which has always been here and will always be here."[10]

The earthly tabernacle of the exodus was "a copy and shadow of what is in heaven" (Hebrews 8:5). John the apostle insinuated that even our bodies are a shadow of substance to come, writing, "Dear friends, now we are children of God, and what we will be has not yet been made known. But we know that when Christ appears, we shall be like him, for we shall see him as he is. All who have this hope in him purify themselves, just as he is pure" (1 John 3:2–3).

Our hope is not in the shadow but the substance. And the substance is Christ, who has gone before us to prepare a new and better place for us, where we will dwell with him forever.

Acknowledgments

Thanks to our student interns who assisted us with this project and for their contributions: Hannah Beckwith Beasley, Kristi Briggs, Leah Holder Green, and Brittany Mann.

Notes

How to Get the Most out of a Discover Together Bible Study

1. William D. Hendricks and Howard Hendricks, *Living by the Book: The Art and Science of Reading the Bible* (Moody, 2007), 23.

Why Study Hebrews?

1. Charles R. Swindoll, *Insights on Hebrews*, Swindoll's Living Insights New Testament Commentary (Tyndale House, 2017), 3.
2. Eusebius, *Ecclesiastical History* 6.25.14.
3. William Simmons, "Nero, Emperor, History of in the Primary Sources," in *The Lexham Bible Dictionary*, ed. John D. Barry et al. (Lexham Press, 2016), https://biblia.com/books/lbd/word/nero.
4. Suetonius, *Lives of the Caesars*, trans. J. C. Rolfe, vol. 2, Loeb Classical Library 38 (Harvard University Press, 1914), 95.

Lesson 1

1. Dana Harris, *Hebrews*, Exegetical Guide to the Greek New Testament, ed. Andreas J. Köstenberger and Robert W. Yarbrough (B&H Academic, 2019), 5.
2. R. Albert Mohler Jr., *Exalting Jesus in Hebrews*, Christ-Centered Exposition Commentary, ed. David Platt, Daniel L. Akin, and Tony Merida (Holman Bible, 2017), 11.
3. Jewish Virtual Library, "Angels and Angelology," accessed April 11, 2024, www.jewishvirtuallibrary.org/angels-and-angelology-2.
4. J. Gordon Melton, "New Age Movement," Britannica, accessed June 26, 2024, https://www.britannica.com/topic/New-Age-movement.
5. N. T. Wright, *Hebrews for Everyone*, 2nd ed. (Westminster John Knox, 2004), 9.
6. Nancy Gibbs, "Angels Among Us," *Time*, December 27, 1993, https://content.time.com/time/subscriber/article/0,33009,979893-2,00.html.
7. Mary Drahos, "Angels of the New Age Kind," EWTN Global Catholic Network, accessed April 11, 2024, https://www.ewtn.com/catholicism/library/angels-of-the-new-age-kind-11314.

8. Charles R. Swindoll, *Insights on Hebrews*, Swindoll's Living Insights New Testament Commentary (Tyndale House, 2017), 19.

9. Swindoll, *Hebrews*, 19.

10. Wright, *Hebrews for Everyone*, 11.

11. Stephen Kim, "BE5107: Bible Exposition of Hebrews, General Epistles, and Revelation," (course lecture, Dallas Theological Society, Fall 2021).

12. Irving L. Jensen, *Hebrews: A Self-Study Guide* (Moody, 1990), 23.

13. Max Lucado, *Life Lessons from Hebrews: The Incomparable Christ* (Thomas Nelson, 2018), 57–58.

Lesson 2

1. Max Lucado, *God Came Near: Chronicle of the Christ* (Multnomah, 1988), 23.

2. J. Dwight Pentecost, *Faith that Endures: A Practical Commentary on the Book of Hebrews*, rev. ed. (Kregel, 2000), 60.

3. C. S. Lewis, *The Four Loves* (Harcourt Brace, 1988), 105.

4. Joseph C. Dillow, *The Reign of the Servant Kings: A Study of Eternal Security and the Final Significance of Man* (Schoettle, 1992), 77.

5. Pentecost, *Faith that Endures*, 70.

6. Mark Hitchcock, *The End: A Complete Overview of Bible Prophecy and the End of Days* (Tyndale House, 2012), 44.

7. Charles R. Swindoll, *Insights on Hebrews*, Swindoll's Living Insights New Testament Commentary (Tyndale House, 2017), 42.

Lesson 3

1. Ágnes Zsila, Lynn E. McCutcheon, and Zsolt Demetrovics, "The Association of Celebrity Worship with Problematic Internet Use, Maladaptive Daydreaming, and Desire for Fame," *Journal of Behavior Addictions* 7, no. 3 (2018): 654–64, doi: 10.1556/2006.7.2018.76.

2. John Maltby et al., "Thou Shalt Worship No Other Gods—Unless They Are Celebrities: The Relationship Between Celebrity Worship and Religious Orientation," *Personality and Individual Differences* 32, no. 7 (May 2002): 1157–72, doi: 10.1016/S0191-8869(01)00059-9.

3. N. T. Wright, *Hebrews for Everyone*, 2nd ed. (Westminster John Knox, 2004), 23.

4. Max Lucado, *Life Lessons from Hebrews: The Incomparable Christ* (Thomas Nelson, 2018), 16.

5. Charles R. Swindoll, *Insights on Hebrews*, Swindoll's Living Insights New Testament Commentary (Tyndale House, 2017), 58.

6. Lucado, *Life Lessons from Hebrews*, 17.

7. J. Paul Tanner, "The Epistle to the Hebrews," in *The Grace New Testament Commentary*, ed. Robert N. Wilkin (Grace Evangelical Society, 2010), 2:1044.

8. Zane C. Hodges, *The Gospel Under Siege: Faith and Works in Tension* (Redencion Viva, 1981), 76.

9. F. F. Bruce, *The Epistle to the Hebrews*, New International Commentary on the New Testament (Eerdmans, 1990, 101.

10. Wright, *Hebrews for Everyone*, 25.

11. Swindoll, *Hebrews*, 61.

12. Augustine, *Confessions*, Volume I: Books 1–8, trans. Carolyn J.-B. Hammond, Loeb Classical Library 26 (Harvard University Press, 2014), 3.

13. Lucado, *Life Lessons from Hebrews*, 27.

14. Scott LaPierre, "What Is Sabbath Rest? (Hebrews 4:1–13)," Scott LaPierre Ministries, June 15, 2023, https://www.scottlapierre.org/what-is-sabbath-rest/.

15. Thomas L. Constable, "Notes on Hebrews: 2024 Edition," Sonic Light, PlanoBibleChapel.org, 2024, 70, https://planobiblechapel.org/tcon/notes/pdf/hebrews.pdf.

16. Francis Thompson, "The Hound of Heaven," 1890, public domain.

Lesson 4

1. Charles R. Swindoll, *Insights on Hebrews*, Swindoll's Living Insights New Testament Commentary (Tyndale House, 2017), 72–74.

2. J. Dwight Pentecost, *Faith that Endures: A Practical Commentary on the Book of Hebrews*, rev. ed. (Kregel, 2000), 39.

3. Jen Wilkin, *Women of the Word: How to Study the Bible with Both Our Hearts and Our Minds* (Crossway, 2014), 152.

4. Richard Strauss, *The Joy of Knowing God* (Loizeaux Brothers, 1984), 133.

5. Max Lucado, *Life Lessons from Hebrews: The Incomparable Christ* (Thomas Nelson, 2018), 36–37.

6. Irving L. Jensen, *Hebrews: A Self-Study Guide* (Moody, 1990), 38.

7. Henri J. M. Nouwen, *A Restless Soul: Meditations from the Road*, ed. Michael Ford (Ave Maria Press, 2008), 19.

8. John Stott, *The Incomparable Christ* (InterVarsity Press, 2001), 89.

9. Philip Yancey, *What's So Amazing About Grace?*, rev. ed. (Zondervan, 2023), 198.

10. William Barclay, *The Letter to the Hebrews*, The New Daily Study Bible (Westminster John Knox, 2002), 63.

11. Swindoll, *Hebrews*, 82.

Lesson 5

1. Charles R. Swindoll, *Insights on Hebrews*, Swindoll's Living Insights New Testament Commentary (Tyndale House, 2017), 106.

2. William G. Moorehead, "Type," in *The International Standard Bible Encyclopedia*, ed. James Orr, John L. Nuelsen, and E. Y. Mullins (Hendrickson, 1994), 4:3029.

3. Swindoll, *Hebrews*, 108.

4. N. T. Wright, *Hebrews for Everyone*, 2nd ed. (Westminster John Knox, 2004), 72.

5. Max Lucado, *In the Grip of Grace: Your Father Always Caught You. He Still Does* (Thomas Nelson, 2011), 72.

6. Thomas L. Constable, "Notes on Hebrews: 2024 Edition," Sonic Light, PlanoBibleChapel.org, 2024, 137, https://planobiblechapel.org/tcon/notes/pdf/hebrews.pdf.

7. Irving L. Jensen, *Hebrews: A Self-Study Guide* (Moody, 1990), 39.

8. Swindoll, *Hebrews*, 123.

9. J. Dwight Pentecost, *Faith that Endures: A Practical Commentary on the Book of Hebrews*, rev. ed. (Kregel, 2000), 48.

Lesson 6

1. Paul Tautges, "In Christ, We Have Direct Access to God," Counseling One Another, May 4, 2022, https://counselingoneanother.com/2022/05/04/in-christ-we-have-direct-access-to-god/.

2. William Strickland, "3 Proven Ways to Take Advantage of Your Access to God," williamstricklandblog.com, November 26, 2020, williamstricklandblog.com/2020/11/26/3-easy-ways-to-take-advantage-of-your-access-to-god/.

3. Irving L. Jensen, *Hebrews: A Self-Study Guide* (Moody, 1990), 71.

4. Jensen, *Hebrews*, 78.

5. Charles R. Swindoll, *Insights on Hebrews*, Swindoll's Living Insights New Testament Commentary (Tyndale House, 2017), 135.

6. Richard J. Foster, *Prayer: Finding the Heart's True Home* (Harper-Collins, 1992), 13.

7. N. T. Wright, *Hebrews for Everyone*, 2nd ed. (Westminster John Knox, 2004), 102–3.

8. Andrew A. Bonar, *Memoir and Remains of Robert Murray M'Cheyne* (Banner of Truth, 1966), in Blue Letter Bible, "If I Could Hear Christ Praying for Me . . ." *The BLB Blog*, November 11, 2011, https://blogs.blueletterbible.org/blb/2011/11/21/if-i-could-here-christ-praying-for-me.

9. Jennifer Kennedy Dean, *Heart's Cry: Principles of Prayer* (New Hope, 1993), 7.

10. Swindoll, *Hebrews*, 142.

11. Dean, *Heart's Cry*, 7.

12. Wright, *Hebrews for Everyone*, 92.

13. Swindoll, *Hebrews*, 152.

14. Jennifer Kennedy Dean, *The Praying Life: Living Beyond Your Limits* (New Hope, 1997), 22–23.

15. John White, *The Fight: A Practical Handbook for Christian Living* (Inter-Varsity Press, 1976), 22.

16. Priscilla Shirer, *Discerning the Voice of God: How to Recognize When God Speaks* (Lifeway, 2006), 6.

Lesson 7

1. John White, *Daring to Draw Near: People in Prayer* (InterVarsity Press, 1977), 129.
2. Jennifer Kennedy Dean, *Heart's Cry: Principles of Prayer* (New Hope, 1997), 8.
3. Max Lucado, *Life Lessons from Hebrews: The Incomparable Christ* (Thomas Nelson, 2018), 57.
4. Julie A. Gorman, *Community That Is Christian: A Handbook on Small Groups*, 2nd ed. (Baker Books, 2002), 12.
5. Heather Zempel, *Community Is Messy: The Perils and Promise of Small Group Ministry* (InterVarsity, 2012), 45.
6. Thomas L. Constable, "Notes on Hebrews: 2024 Edition," Sonic Light, PlanoBibleChapel.org, 2024, 181, https://planobiblechapel.org/tcon/notes/pdf/hebrews.pdf.
7. Constable, "Notes on Hebrews."
8. Charles R. Swindoll, *Insights on Hebrews*, Swindoll's Living Insights New Testament Commentary (Tyndale House, 2017), 161.
9. Swindoll, *Hebrews*, 161.
10. Lucado, *Life Lessons from Hebrews*, x.
11. "Meditation XVII," in *The Works of John Donne*, ed. Henry Alford (John W. Parker, 1839), 3:574–75.
12. Charles Spurgeon, *Spurgeon Commentary: Hebrews*, ed. Elliot Ritzema and Jessi Strong, Spurgeon Commentary Series (Lexham, 2014), 316.
13. William Barclay, *The Letter to the Hebrews*, The New Daily Study Bible (Westminster John Knox, 2002), 154.

Lesson 8

1. Sue Edwards, *Daddy's Girls: Discover the Wonder of the Father* (Kregel, 2007), 22.
2. C. S. Lewis, *The Problem of Pain: How Human Suffering Raises Almost Intolerable Intellectual Problems* (MacMillan, 1962), 93.
3. Charles R. Swindoll, *Insights on Hebrews*, Swindoll's Living Insights New Testament Commentary (Tyndale House, 2017), 196.
4. N. T. Wright, *Hebrews for Everyone*, 2nd ed. (Westminster John Knox, 2004), 153.
5. John Piper, "Glorifying God in Unshakeable Grief," July 11, 2017, in *Ask Pastor John*, Desiring God, https://www.desiringgod.org/interviews/glorifying-god-in-unshakable-grief.
6. Swindoll, *Hebrews*, 199.

7. David L. Allen, *Hebrews*, New American Commentary, vol. 35 (B&H, 2010), 590–91.

8. Charles Spurgeon, *Spurgeon Commentary: Hebrews*, ed. Elliot Ritzema and Jessi Strong, Spurgeon Commentary Series (Lexham, 2014), 436.

Lesson 9

1. Charles R. Swindoll, *Insights on Hebrews*, Swindoll's Living Insights New Testament Commentary (Tyndale House, 2017), 9.

2. William Barclay, *The Letter to the Hebrews*, The New Daily Study Bible (Westminster John Knox, 2002), 225.

3. Charles Spurgeon, *Spurgeon Commentary: Hebrews*, ed. Elliot Ritzema and Jessi Strong, Spurgeon Commentary Series (Lexham, 2014), 445.

4. N. T. Wright, *Hebrews for Everyone*, 2nd ed. (Westminster John Knox, 2004), 170.

5. Spurgeon, *Hebrews*, 458.

6. Dennis E. Johnson, "Hebrews," in *ESV Expository Commentary*, ed. Ian M. Duguid, James M. Hamilton Jr., and Jay Sklar (Crossway, 2018), 12:208.

7. Mark Hitchcock, *The End: A Complete Overview of Bible Prophecy and the End of Days* (Tyndale, 2012), xi.

8. Chris Tiegreen, *The One Year Praying in Faith Devotional* (Tyndale Momentum, 2021), 283.

9. Max Lucado, *Life Lessons from Hebrews: The Incomparable Christ* (Thomas Nelson, 2018), 118–19.

10. C. S. Lewis, *The Last Battle*, in *The Complete Chronicles of Narnia* (HarperCollins, 1998), 519.

About the Authors

Sue Edwards is professor emeritus of educational ministries and leadership (her specialization is women's studies) at Dallas Theological Seminary (DTS), where she has had the opportunity to equip men and women for future ministry. She brought more than forty years of experience into the classroom as a Bible teacher, curriculum writer, and overseer of several megachurch women's ministries. Ministering to women at two megachurches in Dallas, she has worked with women from all walks of life, ages, and stages. Her passion is to see modern and postmodern women connect, learn from one another, and bond around God's Word. Her Bible studies have ushered thousands of women—all over the country and overseas—into deeper Scripture study and community experiences.

With Kelley Mathews, Sue has coauthored *Organic Ministry to Women: A Guide to Transformational Ministry with Next Generation Women* and *Leading Women Who Wound: Strategies for an Effective Ministry*. Sue and Kelley joined with Henry J. Rogers to coauthor *Mixed Ministry: Working Together as Brothers and Sisters in an Oversexed Society*. *Organic Mentoring: A Mentor's Guide to Relationships with Next Generation Women*, coauthored with Barbara Neumann, explores the new values, preferences, and problems of the next generation and shows mentors how to avoid potential land mines and how to mentor successfully. She coedited *Invitation to Educational Ministry: Foundations of Transformative Christian Education* with the DTS vice president for education and professor of educational ministries and leadership, George M. Hillman Jr. This book serves as a primary academic textbook for schools all over the country as well as a handbook for church leaders. Sue teamed up again with Kelley to write their newest book, *40 Questions About Women in Ministry*, released in 2023, which in 2024 received the Editor's Choice Award from the Christian Editors Association and was a finalist for the ECPA Christian Book Award in the category of Ministry Resources.

Sue earned a doctor of ministry degree from Gordon-Conwell Theological Seminary in Boston, a master's in Bible from DTS, and a bachelor's degree in journalism from Trinity University. With Dr. Joye Baker, she oversees the DTS doctor of ministry degree in educational ministry with a women-in-ministry emphasis.

Sue has been married to David for fifty-three years. They have two married daughters, Heather and Rachel, and five grandchildren. David is a retired CAD applications engineer and a lay prison chaplain. Sue loves fine chocolates and exotic coffees, conversations with her grandchildren, and taking walks with David and their two West Highland terriers, Quigley and Mitzi.

Rebecca Carrell is a Bible teacher, conference speaker, and author. She speaks all over the country, challenging women to become biblically literate and all-in Christ-followers. After spending over twenty years as a morning radio host in Dallas–Fort Worth, she now mentors, ministers to, and instructs students at Dallas Theological Seminary (DTS) in the educational ministries & leadership and the media arts & worship departments. She earned her bachelor of science in journalism at the University of Kansas and her master of arts in educational ministry & leadership from DTS and is currently working toward her doctorate.

Rebecca hosts and produces two podcasts: *The Story of Scripture Podcast* with DTS President Dr. Mark Yarbrough and Dr. Josh Winn, and *Honestly, Though: Real Talk. Real Life. Real Faith.* Her books include *Holy Jellybeans: Finding God through Everyday Things*; *Holy Hiking Boots: When God Makes the Ordinary Extraordinary*, and *Anxious for Nothing: Paul's Letter to the Philippians*.

She and her husband Mike have been married for over twenty years and live in the Dallas–Fort Worth area with their two (almost) grown children, Caitlyn and Nick. Connect with Rebecca on X, Instagram, Facebook, or through www.rebeccacarrell.com.

Organic
MENTORING

A MENTOR'S
GUIDE TO
RELATIONSHIPS
WITH NEXT
GENERATION
WOMEN

SUE EDWARDS & BARBARA NEUMANN

"I love this book! I will definitely incorporate it into several contexts, including my seminary classroom teaching as well as personal relationships. Generational differences have clearly stalled the mentoring advantage. *Organic Mentoring* gets us moving again in a world that desperately needs the benefit of intergenerational mentoring."

—BEV HISLOP, Professor of Pastoral Care, Western Seminary, and author of *Shepherding a Woman's Heart* and *Shepherding Women in Pain*

KREGEL
MINISTRY

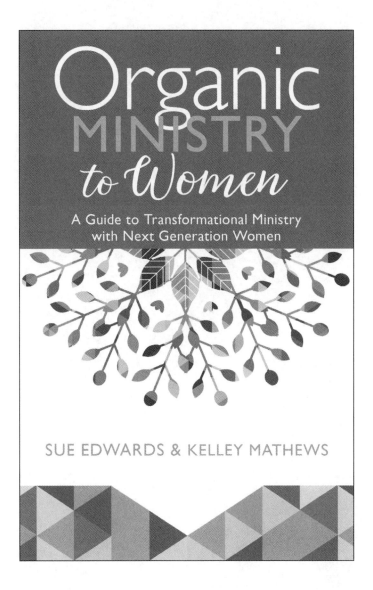

Drawing on decades of experience ministering to women, authors Sue Edwards and Kelley Mathews explain how their Transformation Model can energize women's ministry for all generations and in multiple settings. *Organic Ministry to Women* is packed with practical advice and real-life illustrations of how to implement the principles of the Transformation Model. Edwards and Mathews also profile numerous leading women's ministers like Jen Wilkin, Priscilla Shirer, and Jackie Hill-Perry, drawing wisdom and inspiration from their lives and ministries. Helpful appendixes provide additional resources including sample job descriptions for ministry leaders, a Bible study lesson, and a training guide for small group leaders.

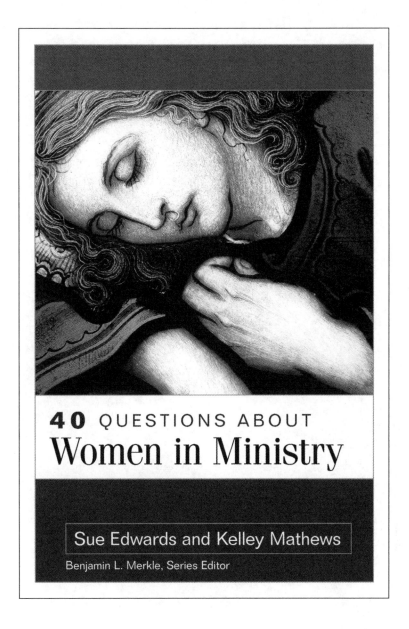

40 QUESTIONS ABOUT
Women in Ministry

Sue Edwards and Kelley Mathews

Benjamin L. Merkle, Series Editor

40 Questions About Women in Ministry charts a course for understanding differing views on the topic. The accessible question-and-answer format guides readers through specific areas of confusion, and the authors helpfully zero in on the foundations of varied beliefs and practices. Sue Edwards and Kelley Mathews cover interpretive, theological, historical, and practical matters, such as, What did God mean by the woman as man's "helper"? How is it that Christians reach different conclusions about 1 Timothy 2:11–15? How did Western culture influence women's roles in society and the church?

KREGEL
ACADEMIC